exodus 24-40

A **SIMPLY BIBLE** STUDY

CARMEN BEASLEY

Copyright © 2023 | by Carmen Beasley

All rights reserved. No part of this publication may be reproduced, distributed, or transmitted in any form or by any means, including photocopying, recording, or other electronic or mechanical methods, without the prior written permission of the publisher, except in the case of brief quotations embodied in critical reviews and certain other noncommercial uses permitted by copyright law.

Scripture quotations are from the ESV® Bible (The Holy Bible, English Standard Version®), copyright © 2001 by Crossway, a publishing ministry of Good News Publishers. Used by permission. All rights reserved.

Journal and layout design by Melissa Trew.

To our LORD.

That all may know Your grace.

I am the LORD your God, who brought you out of the land of Egypt, out of the house of slavery.

EXODUS 20:2

The LORD passed before him and proclaimed, "The LORD, the LORD, a God merciful and gracious, slow to anger, and abounding in steadfast love and faithfulness…"

EXODUS 34:6

I WILL DWELL AMONG
THE PEOPLE OF ISRAEL AND
WILL BE THEIR GOD.

EXODUS 29:45

table of *contents*

EXODUS 24-40 | A **SIMPLY BIBLE** STUDY

INTRODUCTION

I.	**Welcome to Exodus** | Redemption that Reveals God's Heart	1
II.	**Inductive Study** | An Introduction to SIMPLY BIBLE	9
III.	**Getting Started** | A Quick-Start Guide	13
IV.	**Step by Step** | Unpacking the Inductive Method	17
V.	**Lesson Samples** | Practice Lessons & Examples	27
VI.	**In Context** | Examining the Context of Exodus	37
VII.	**A Challenge** | Know & Enjoy the God of the Old Testament	45

STUDY CONTENT

I.	**Exodus 24**	51
II.	**Exodus 25 & 26**	67
III.	**Exodus 27 & 28**	87
IV.	**Exodus 29 & 30**	107
V.	**Exodus 31 & 32**	127
VI.	**Exodus 33 & 34**	145
VII.	**Exodus 35 & 36**	165
VIII.	**Exodus 37 & 38**	185
IX.	**Exodus 39 & 40**	205
X.	**Final Thoughts** | Wrapping Up	225

APPENDIX

I.	**Leader Guide** | Maximizing the Small Group Experience	233

welcome

REDEMPTION THAT REVEALS GOD'S HEART

welcome to *exodus*

REDEMPTION THAT REVEALS GOD'S HEART

A *flashback* is a technique used in movies, novels, and other narratives in which the present story transitions into a scene from the past. When used as a verb, the term is usually spelled as two words, as in *My favorite part of the book is when it flashes back to their childhood.* The opposite of a *flashback* is a flash-forward—when the narrative transitions into a scene from the future. [1]

Back to the Future is the first movie my hubby and I saw as a married couple, just weeks after our wedding. (Yep. That dates me.) As the title suggests, the movie utilizes flashback. The main character—a California teen named Marty McFly, played by Michael J. Fox— ends up going back in time to the 1950s, with the help of a mad scientist named Doc Brown, played by Christopher Lloyd. Humorously, while back in time, Marty encounters his own parents as teenagers.

Doc's experiment goes hilariously awry, such that Marty desperately needs to flash-forward *back to the future.* As all good stories go, all's well that ends well, and conflict resolution happens in the end. The movie cleverly utilizes flashback and flash-forward to create a highly entertaining movie. According to Wikipedia, *Back to the Future* was the most successful and highest-grossing film during the year 1985. [2]

Vividly remembering a past time or utilizing the present to point to the future are powerful tools to connect a story from beginning to end. Flashing back and flashing forward proved successful in *Back to the Future.* Flashing back and flashing forward work similarly in the Bible.

---

[1] **flashback**. Dictionary.com. *Dictionary.com Unabridged.* Random House, Inc. http://www.dictionary.com/browse/flashback (accessed: Feb. 2023).

[2] *Back to the Future.* Wikipedia. https://en.wikipedia.org/Back_to_the_Future (accessed: Feb. 2023).

WHY STUDY THE BOOK OF EXODUS?

Flashing back within the Bible's historical storyline powerfully connects us to God. A flashback to Exodus reveals God's ultimate power, but also displays God's divine character and heart. In Exodus, we find a God of compassion.

When He hears the cry of His suffering people, grace and faithfulness emanate from deep within. He is moved to act on their behalf to rescue. Yet, if we slow down to ponder the Exodus narrative, we will also find God's heart of grace, not only for His people, but also for the Egyptians; a heart that provides opportunity upon opportunity for them to know Him and turn from their evil ways.

Many of us hold a false perception of God as being a harsh and ruthless tyrant who smites humans on a whim, particularly the God of the Old Testament. If God were to write His own introduction, some might imagine Him writing something along these lines:

> "I am the LORD. I created the heavens and the earth and rule over all. There is no other God like me. Follow me with Your whole heart or I will pummel You with my iron fist."

This idea paints a false picture of God's heart. Yes, He is LORD. Yes, He created the heavens and the earth. Yes, He rules over all. Yes, He desires our hearts and affection. But Exodus reveals that God's heart is tender and very different from a God or a Pharaoh eager to smite people. The fact of the matter is that, within Exodus, God does share His own introductory bio. Are you curious about how God describes Himself?

> "The LORD, the LORD, a God merciful and gracious, slow to anger, and abounding in steadfast love and faithfulness, keeping steadfast love for thousands, forgiving iniquity and transgression and sin, but who will by no means clear the guilty, visiting the iniquity of the fathers on the children and the children's children, to the third and the fourth generation."
>
> EXODUS 34:6-7

Surprised? Unlike Pharoah, God does not boast of His power and might, but rather, He fully discloses His heart: a tender and humble heart of compassion and goodness. He describes Himself as merciful, gracious, slow to anger, and abounding in steadfast love and kindness. His Word is true, such that His heart stirs and propels Him to act.

Yes! He will set His people free. Yes! He will deliver the captives from bondage. Yes! He will rescue His own from the chains of death. Not because there is anything special about these people. Rather, it has everything to do with His extraordinary heart. A heart that also extends grace to the oppressors.

THIS IS THE TRUE GOD OF THE OLD TESTAMENT. He does not change:

> For I the LORD do not change; therefore you, O children of Jacob, are not consumed.
>
> MALACHI 3:6

Because this God remains unchanged, we find the same powerful God when flashing-forward to the New Testament. Through Jesus, the Lamb of God Who takes away the sins of the world, God sets His people free, rescuing them from the bondage of sin and death through the blood of the Passover Lamb, His Son. Once again, God's rescue mission emanates from His unchanged heart of compassion, grace, and love for His people. He acts on their behalf in order to connect with His people.

Whether we flash forward or flash back in the Bible, we find the same powerful God, with the same heart of compassion, who acts to deliver His people from bondage. To be ultra-clear, consider the following similarities as we prepare to know and experience God through the powerful story of Exodus. The exodus of God's people from bondage and death endures as the leading event of the Old Testament. Here we find:

(1) God rescues Israel from bondage through the blood of the Passover lamb.

(2) He then delivers them from death at the crossing of the Red Sea.

(3) Knowing that His people have been captives in Egypt and need clarity to manage their newfound freedom, God provides detailed instructions on how to rightly live and worship Him.

(4) Ultimately, the Mount Sinai laws make the way clear: **love** God and **love** one another.

This pattern in Exodus points forward to the future events of the New Testament:

(1) Through Christ's death on the cross as the Lamb of God Who takes away the sins of the world, God rescues His people.

(2) Jesus then conquers death by His resurrection from the grave.

(3) With newfound freedom as believers in Jesus, how shall God's people live? Knowing that His people have been captive to sin and death, much of the New Testament clearly explains how we ought to rightly live and worship God, bearing His heart of love.

(4) The way is clear, and once again, God's Word flashes back to Exodus: **love** God and **love** others.

Whichever direction we journey in the Bible—a flashback or a flash-forward—God reveals much about Himself and His heart. His heart remains the same yesterday, today, and tomorrow. God desires to be known and to be united with His people. He stops at nothing to make this happen. He utilizes His mighty power to bring life out of death so that we might know and trust Him.

Friend, are you groaning in the midst of great trials or weary with heavy burdens? Do you feel alone, afraid, lost, or anxious about tomorrow?

WELCOME TO EXODUS. This flashback into the Old Testament displays a God Who sees, hears, and knows His people. Out of the essence of His heart, He moves powerfully on their behalf. God remains every bit as compassionate toward those in bondage today as He was to the Israelites of the Ancient Near East. He mightily broke their chains, He holds the same power to break ours as well.

SIMPLY BIBLE | **EXODUS** guides us on a journey to better know and enjoy this God. God gifted us with hearts to engage directly with His heart. Hearts purposed to worship Him. And He is worthy of it. He alone claims the Name, "I AM Who I AM." Together we will marvel at Him, His works, and enjoy the essence of His character. For hearts and minds weary and burdened, this study will refresh our souls.

Whether we flash forward or flashback in the Bible, God beckons:

> Come to me, all who labor and are heavy laden, and I will give you rest.
>
> MATTHEW 11:28

Friend, full disclosure here: the journey through Exodus is not a short one. In order to work our way through 40 chapters, this study has been divided into three books. Each provides a window to a greater understanding of our God and His heart of mercy.

Briefly, here is why each of the three books is important:

Book 1 | Exodus 1-12
The LORD rescues. Call it redemption. Call it deliverance. We see God break the chains of His people and set them free.

Book 2 | Exodus 13-23
The LORD provides. Outside of Egypt, God has the back of His people. He miraculously brings life out of death at the Red Sea. He keeps them safe and provides for their needs in the wilderness.

Book 3 | Exodus 24-40
The LORD is present with His people. Footloose and fancy free, how should God's people live? How will God be worshipped? God graciously gives instructions.

In order to keep it simple, each book of the SIMPLY BIBLE | **EXODUS** series is laid out in exactly the same way. This includes the same introduction and challenge. This repetition is purposeful and is intended to help us better know and enjoy the God of Exodus. The only variance within the books are the chapters of Scripture studied.

I'm grateful you've joined SIMPLY BIBLE on this journey. Together, let's commit to knowing and enjoying God through Exodus. As we do, my prayer is that we will discover our purpose—our very reason for living and breathing and singing—to have faith and to worship the LORD, Who remains merciful and gracious, slow to anger, and abounding in steadfast love forever and ever. Oh! May hearts be encouraged!

With much joy,

Carmen

PS—For more Bible study tips, please visit and join our online community at **www.simplybiblestudy.org**.

simply bible
AN INDUCTIVE BIBLE STUDY

After her first study, a friend described SIMPLY BIBLE as "leaving behind her paint by numbers set for a blank canvas." Whether painting, drawing, or digging into God's Word, using a blank canvas can be a little intimidating. It takes practice! Just as artists learn a particular method and handle special tools to create a masterpiece, so do Bible study students.

The methodology utilized within SIMPLY BIBLE is known as *inductive study*. This method is used by Bible scholars, pastors, teachers, and students of all levels, and can easily be completed using a Bible and plain notebook. Frankly, the SIMPLY BIBLE workbooks are not necessary for inductive study. However, most readers agree that these user-friendly guides simplify and ease the study process by providing everything needed in one place via an easy-to-follow, logical format.

The inductive method involves three basic steps that often overlap with one another:
   (1) Observe
   (2) Interpret
   (3) Apply

This three-step format helps to paint a more thorough understanding of God's Word.

On the following pages, you will find A QUICK-START GUIDE TO **SIMPLY BIBLE**. Bookmark and use this as needed. The quick-start guide is followed by a more thorough explanation of the format and basic study tools. Take time to get a feel for each step. Read the examples. And then, dig in!

inductive study

AN INTRODUCTION TO **SIMPLY BIBLE**

inductive bible study
AN INTRODUCTION TO **SIMPLY BIBLE**

AS A LITTLE GIRL, I ADORED COLORING BOOKS. Smooth, crisp white pages displayed bold black lines of perfectly-drawn figures and characters. The spaces patiently awaited color. Fondly, I remember the joy of opening a new pack of crayons. The waxy smell and the neat little rows of pointed tips colorfully peeked out and tantalized me as if to say, "Try to choose just one!" Creativity awaited. Or so I thought.

When my four children were small, a friend of a friend encouraged me to forgo purchasing coloring books and simply provide them with plain, white paper. My initial reaction was one of horror. "What? Coloring books are fun! That would be forgoing fun! Plain paper? How boring!" Okay, granted… my reaction was a little melodramatic, but I do remember thinking these thoughts.

Instead, this friend insisted that providing children with blank sheets of paper was the way to spur creativity. I could see the wisdom. Not to mention, a ream of paper was way cheaper than four new coloring books… and so, I gave it a try. Does this mean I never gave my children coloring books? No! My children certainly enjoyed a few coloring books here and there. However, I admit that these books never seemed to offer my children the same kind of joy that coloring books had offered me. And so, for the most part, my children simply grew up with lots of plain white paper and a variety of colorful pencils, crayons, and markers.

PLAIN, WHITE PAPER IT WAS. What happened? My kids learned to draw. Not just little stick figures in the middle of the page, but they learned to tell a story using a piece of paper. Masterpieces. (So this mom deems them.)

Now, I'm sure no one ever saved one of my coloring book pages. Oh, for sure! Sometimes one landed on Grandma's refrigerator. However, right now, down in my basement, there remain binders of pictures that my budding artists created twenty years ago.

Why? These pictures were windows into their little souls and minds. For example, if God was not present in a Bible story, my son would draw a big eye in the sky. In his little five-year-old heart, he understood that God could see him. Had I handed my children coloring book pages where they filled in the blanks, I would never have had this window into their hearts and minds.

Their works of art tell stories. And I treasure them in my heart.

THIS IS THE GIST OF **SIMPLY BIBLE**. These guides provide a "blank page" for reading and directly engaging with God and His Word. Rather than fill-in-the-blank questions, SIMPLY BIBLE offers space to be curious and ask your own questions. You will learn to observe, understand, and apply. Don't get me wrong: just like coloring books, traditional Bible studies have their place. Without them, I wouldn't be the Bible student that I am today. And yet, I am rather fond of this SIMPLY BIBLE series. With gentle direction, these books allow quiet spaces for listening to and knowing God, relating with Him by sharing in His story: *simply the Bible*.

Since its inception, I've known the joy and privilege of watching others seek God through SIMPLY BIBLE. I've watched these Bible study journals become windows into hearts, souls, and minds growing with God. These workbooks tell personal stories. And although the stories are often much too private for me to observe closely, I treasure each one in my heart. If I could, I'd pile them up in my basement. Perhaps it's cheesy, but in some tender way, they seem piled up in the "basement of my heart."

Finally, I want to thank Melissa Trew. SIMPLY BIBLE would not be the same without her. As a gifted designer, she takes ordinary ideas and transforms them into extraordinarily beautiful workbooks. Coffee-table-worthy. Melissa, I am eternally grateful. Thank you.

SO WELCOME TO **SIMPLY BIBLE**! The rest of the introduction provides step-by-step guidance on getting started with the inductive Bible study method. You'll find everything you need to know to engage directly with God and His Word. Please read these sections before beginning the study.

"THE LORD, THE LORD, A GOD MERCIFUL AND GRACIOUS, SLOW TO ANGER, AND ABOUNDING IN STEADFAST LOVE AND FAITHFULNESS..."

EXODUS 34:6

getting *started*

A QUICK-START GUIDE

getting *started*

A QUICK-START GUIDE

READ	OBSERVE	INTERPRET
Read the passage. Try some or all of these ideas to help you read carefully. (Highlighters and colored pencils are fun here!) • Read the passage in a different version. • Read it out loud. • Underline, circle, box, or highlight repeated words, unfamiliar words, or anything that pricks your heart or catches your attention. • Listen to the passage while running errands. • Doodle or write out a verse in your workbook or a journaling Bible.	As you read, write down your observations in this column. Simply notice what the Scripture *says*. This is your place for notes. Ideas include: • Ask questions of the text, like "who, what, when, where, or how." • Jot down key items: people, places, things. Mark places on a map. • Ask, "What does this passage say about God? Jesus? Holy Spirit?" • Note what took place before and after this passage. • Ponder. • Ask God if there is anything else He'd like you to notice.	In this column, record what the passage *means*. One way to interpret is to answer any questions asked during observation. Try to first answer these *without* the aid of other helps. Allow Scripture to explain Scripture. It often does. If the answers are not intuitive or easily found near the passage, other tools are available. Use boxes A, B, and C to identify a key word, define it, and look up a cross reference. This extra research will shed light on the meaning. IMPORTANT: *Seek to understand what the passage meant to Moses and to his original readers (or hearers). Try to see and look at the world through the eyes of the Ancient Near East culture of the day.*

PLEASE NOTE: The following boxes (labeled A, B, and C) are interpretation tools. These are meant to be used in unison with the "Interpret" column on the previous page to aid in interpreting Scripture. Most students find it helpful to complete these before interpreting. Consider this your toolbox. Find what's most helpful for you.

A KEY WORDS	B DEFINITIONS	C CROSS REFERENCES
When you notice a word that is repeated multiple times, unfamiliar, or interesting to you in any other way, record it here.	Record definitions of your key words. You can find the appropriate definitions by using: • a Bible concordance (defines words according to the original language) • a Bible dictionary • another translation	Note cross references. This is a solid way to allow Scripture to interpret Scripture. If your Bible does not include cross references, they can be found easily using online resources.

Bible study tools like those listed above can be found by visiting the following websites:

blueletterbible.org **biblegateway.com** **biblehub.com**

logos.org **stepbible.org**

MAIN POINTS	APPLY
Summarize the main point(s) or note any themes you encountered in the passage.	Apply God's Word specifically to your own life. Application is personal. God may teach, correct, rebuke, or train. He is always equipping. (II Tim. 3:16-17) Record what the passage means to you.

PRAY

Write a short prayer here. When we take time to write something down, that message becomes more etched on our heart. Take a moment to simply be with God. He is why we study. Savor. Know. Praise. Confess. Thank. Ask. Love. Then carry a nugget of His Word in your heart to ponder and proclaim throughout your day.

> YOU SHALL ERECT THE TABERNACLE ACCORDING TO THE PLAN FOR IT THAT YOU WERE SHOWN ON THE MOUNTAIN.
>
> EXODUS 26:30

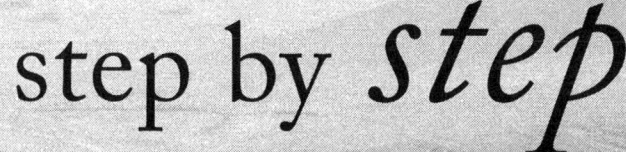

step by *step*

UNPACKING THE INDUCTIVE METHOD

step by *step*
UNPACKING THE INDUCTIVE METHOD

STEP 1: OBSERVE | *See what the Bible **says**.*

The first step of Bible study is to observe God's Word.

In our hurried, scurried pace of life, we read too fast, often plowing through the words without taking time to ponder and think about what we're reading. *Observation* helps us to slow down and take notice in order to see. In this first step, we answer, "What does the Bible *say*?"

Have you ever stopped to truly examine and enjoy a piece of art? Artists develop an amazing knack or ability to capture a particular scene, whether real or imagined, onto a blank canvas. How? Artists specialize in observing details: setting, color, texture, time, characters, lighting, movement… The list of details is nearly limitless.

We can, too.

When my children were younger, blank sketch books and new drawing pencils equaled a special treat. With fresh, new artist tools in hand and a sunny day, my little ones and I would traipse excitedly through a park. Before pulling out a pencil to begin creating, we needed to find the right spot for observing. (I highly recommend that for Bible study, too!)

To observe means "to see, watch, notice, or regard with attention, especially so as to see or learn something."[1] *Especially so as to see or learn something.*

---

[1] **observe**. Dictionary.com. *Dictionary.com Unabridged.* Random House, Inc. http://www.dictionary.com/browse/observe (accessed: March 16, 2018).

And so, my children and I would notice things. Lots of things… the different types of leaves, flowers, plants, grass, insects, animals, and more. Once engaged in observing, details would begin to arise! How fun to zero in and observe the ladybug crawling along the blade of grass or the spots that adorn a toad sunning on the sidewalk or the veins that run throughout a maple leaf. There's so much to see!

Observation implies being curious. Noticing details. Asking questions.

Kids do this naturally. We can too. Be curious with God's Word. Scripture is full of details to notice and numerous questions to ask. When we slow down and take time to "smell the roses" within Scripture, we see and learn.

If you don't relate to art or being a kid again, then consider detective work. Inductive study is much like detective work. Detectives are trained to observe and notice details. They exude curiosity and examine cases by asking questions: who, what, when, where, how, and why.

Like detectives, we use observation skills too. Intuitively, without even thinking about it, we observe and interpret life around us.

Consider a family member or roommate. Using simple observation, we discern whether a loved one comes home happy, sad, or mad. After all, there's a huge difference between walking through the door with a smile or a frown. Singing a tune versus grumbling. Dancing versus slamming doors. We notice the "signs." And because we care, we ask questions. Inquisitive minds want to know, "What's up?" This leads to more questions: "Really? How? Why? Where? When? Who? Are you okay?" You get the picture.

Detective work transfers to reading and understanding God's Word. Observation means we read, study, and ask questions of the text. We look to see, "What does the Scripture say?" If short on time, we simply ask, "What does the Scripture say about who God is?"

As you read, pray and talk with God about His Word. Ask Him to help you see. Ask Him questions about the text. Highlight verses that touch your heart. If anything is especially noteworthy to you, jot it down in the space labeled **Observe** in your workbook. (Keep in mind: the SIMPLY BIBLE framework is just a guide. You choose to fill in as little or as much as you desire.)

The bottom line? Read. Read carefully. Observe at least one thing, particularly something about God Himself. This allows us to see Scripture more clearly.

STEP 2: INTERPRET | *Understand what the Scripture **means**.*

After careful observation of a landscape, an artist sketches an interpretation of what he sees onto the canvas. Observation and interpretation go hand in hand. A circle is a circle. A square is a square. As closely as possible, the artist defines and places an image of what he observes onto the canvas. Careful observation leads to a life-like rendering such that the viewer will understand what the artist himself observed.

The same is true of the Bible. Observation and interpretation go hand in hand. Scripture will often interpret Scripture. As we carefully read and observe what the scripture says, we frequently understand and simultaneously interpret it's *meaning*. So within our daily study format, observation and interpretation are located side-by-side.

One simple way to understand the meaning of Scripture is to answer the questions we asked in the observation process: the who, what, where, when, how, and why. Try to answer these questions without the aid of study notes or other helps. Utilize scripture to interpret scripture. Often, the answer is readily available.

Other times, interpretation is not so easy. After all, the Bible was written in ancient times, spanning the course of over two thousand years, *by* a people and *to* a people of a culture that is utterly foreign to us.

Therefore, certain resources are handy. These tools can help us to place and understand Scripture in its original context in order to properly interpret. (Think of an artist using a ruler—a simple tool that helps to more accurately reproduce a scene. A ruler is not necessary, but is useful.)

Bible study tools can include:

- *Cross references:* Cross references allow us to use nearby or related passages to more accurately interpret Scripture.
- *Bible dictionaries or concordances:* These tools allow students to understand the meaning of a word in its original language.
- *Bible handbooks and commentaries:* Resources like these help us to verify our conclusions as well as provide historical or cultural context.

It's important to remember that Scripture, in its original context, had only one meaning. Not multiple meanings. And although our God can be mysterious in His ways, there are no mystical or hidden meanings within Scripture. The author of Exodus wrote a specific message, in a specific time and place, for a specific group of people. He meant what he said. For this study, we want to know what the author *meant* and how the Israelites *understood* his words. Although we may not always be able to determine an author's specific intent, that is our goal.

Interpretation implies understanding. Original meaning and context are important. Be reasonable. Compare.

Seek correct answers, but give yourself grace. A child's rendering of a ladybug on a blade of grass will not equate to Van Gogh's renderings, and yet, there is something wholly precious about the works of a child. Our renderings of Scripture won't ever equate to a Bible scholar's commentary. That is not our goal. Our goal is knowing and enjoying God. Sometimes this involves taking tiny baby steps in His direction.

A, B, & C: TOOLS FOR INTERPRETATION

If the answers are not intuitive or easily found within the passage, tools are available to help us better understand. Our daily lesson format provides three boxes intended to support interpretation. Here, you'll find space to identify key words, define those key words, and record supporting verses (cross references). These are intended to help and guide you as you interpret Scripture. Consider this to be your interpretation toolbox. Use the tools however you find them to be helpful.

> **A.** KEY WORDS | Did you notice that a word was repeated, seems important, is unfamiliar, or interests you in any way? Record it here.
>
> **B.** DEFINITIONS | Use this box to record definitions of the words you listed.
>
> - *Read the verse using a different translation or version of the Bible.* This can be a very simple way to define a word. For example, our practice lesson (on page 28) notes the word *void* from Genesis 1:2. The ESV version says "void," while the NIV translates the Hebrew as "empty."[1]
>
> - *Use a Bible concordance.* This book looks at words in their original language. I like the **Strong's Concordance**, which can also be found online.
>
>   **i.** Going online? Try **Blue Letter Bible**, a free web-based concordance.
>
>   **ii.** Once there, (referring to our practice lesson on page 28) simply type "Genesis 1" into the *Search the Bible* box. Select the box called *Tools* next to Genesis 1:2 and a menu appears. Find and select the corresponding Strong's Concordance number for "void" (in this case: H922). You'll retrieve the Hebrew word, original definitions (void, emptiness, and waste, and where else it is used in Scripture. It's fascinating!

---

[1] The Holy Bible: The Amplified Bible. 1987. La Habra, CA: The Lockman Foundation.

> - *Try a Bible dictionary.* In order to define people or locate places, Bible dictionaries are handy.
>
>   **i.** Online, try **Bible Gateway, Blue Letter Bible, Bible Hub,** or **Logos.**
>
>   **ii.** Wonderful Bible study apps exist, too. For example, the **Bible Map** app is simple-to-use and automatically syncs Scripture with maps.
>
> **C.** CROSS REFERENCES | Many Bibles offer cross references. This is a rock-solid way to allow Scripture to interpret Scripture. If your Bible does not include cross references (most journaling Bibles do not), no worries! Accessing cross references online is easy. **Step Bible, Blue Letter Bible,** or **Bible Hub** are great places to start.

Still not sure?

Note your question and talk to God about it. Ponder. As we ponder Scripture, God often illuminates our understanding. Other times, He allows certain things to remain unanswered. His ways are sometimes beyond our ways and our understanding. Ultimately, we walk by faith.

Remember to share and discuss your questions with others at Bible study. Studying God's Word is meant to be done in community where we learn and grow together in knowing, understanding, and loving God.

WANT MORE? Our daily study format includes space for definitions and cross references. However, there are other Bible study resources available if you'd like to dig even deeper.

Bible commentaries are written by Biblical scholars. These books provide cultural and historical context while commenting on Scripture verse-by-verse.

Personally, I admire the dedication and genius of scholars who write commentaries. These dedicated people study for the glory of God. And yet, I recommend saving their wonderful resources as a last step. Why? Because commentaries are not a substitute for reading, understanding, and engaging God's Word on your own. First seek to understand God's Word without a commentary. Then, if desired, utilize a commentary for double-checking your work.

Also, please note that commentaries are written according to various theological bents. It's helpful to compare. Know your sources. This is especially crucial if roaming the Internet. Please surf with discernment and great care. I can't emphasize this enough. Unfortunately, even commentaries found on popular Bible study sites are not always researched or written by trained Biblical scholars. If unsure, background-check the author's credentials. Bible degrees and scholastic training from accredited universities and institutions are important.

To find reliable Biblical commentaries, I recommend:

> www.bestcommentaries.com   www.challies.com

SUMMARIZE: Your daily framework offers space for you to summarize and identify the main point(s) of the Bible passage you've read. If reading a narrative, consider summarizing the plot. Understanding the main idea of a passage helps to ensure a correct interpretation before moving into application.

STEP 3: APPLY | *Put it all **together**.*

Here's the "So what? How will I think or act differently because of God's Word?" With the Holy Spirit's help, observation and interpretation lead us to better understand the meaning of a Bible passage. That's thrilling! Discovering a nugget of truth, a promise, or a revelation about God Himself takes my breath away and inevitably leads me to praise and worship Him. There is no other book like the Bible:

> For the word of God is living and active,
> sharper than any two-edged sword,
> piercing to the division of soul and of spirit,
> of joints and of marrow, and discerning
> the thoughts and intentions of the heart.
>
> HEBREWS 4:12

The God of the Universe loves us and personally reveals Himself through His Living Word. When He does, it cuts in a good way. Then we're ready to apply His Word to our everyday lives… to *think* and *act* differently.

APPLICATION IS THE CREATIVE PART. Yes, the original author of Scripture had one meaning, but the personal applications of Scripture are many. This step is between you and God. If a specific verse, word, or idea strikes a chord in your heart, *slow down*. Take note. Show God the discovery. This is the amazing process of God revealing Himself and His truths to you through His Word and the power of His Spirit.

God looks at our hearts. He sees, knows, and loves His sheep. And so, He may use His Word to teach, correct, rebuke, or train. He is always equipping (II Timothy 3:16-17). If you're willing, He will lead you to apply His Word specifically to your everyday life.

Application ideas include:
1. Worship God for who He is, according to a truth or promise discovered.
2. Thank Him for a lesson learned.
3. Note an example to follow.
4. Confess a sin revealed.
5. Pray a prayer noticed.
6. Obey, trust, and follow God's way, His command, His plan.
7. Memorize a verse.

Bottom line? Ask yourself, "How will I think or act differently because of what I've learned in God's Word?"

WRAPPING UP: PRAY | *Respond to a **Holy God**.*

Application implies a recognition of who God is. And so, when wrapping up personal study, the application step almost always leads me to bow my heart in worship, confession, or thanksgiving. Sometimes, I recognize a need in my life. Hence, the SIMPLY BIBLE daily format includes a place for *prayer*. Please use this! It may be the most important space of all.

Enjoy a lingering moment of being with God in His Word. Savor. Learn. Grow. Know. Thank. Praise. Confess. Yield. Love. Then carry a nugget of truth in your heart to ponder as you go about your day.

lesson *samples*

PRACTICE LESSONS & EXAMPLES

practice *lesson*

GENESIS 1:1-5

NOW IT'S YOUR TURN! Give it a try! Below are a few verses: Genesis 1:1-5. As you read, feel free to highlight, circle, underline, and mark up the text in whatever way you like. In the *Observe* column, jot down details that pop out and write down questions that come to mind. Then *Interpret*. Simply use the Scripture itself or hop over to the toolkit of *Key Words*, *Definitions*, and *Cross References*. Use these as previously discussed to help you better understand the meaning. Finish by summarizing, applying, and praying.

This is your workbook. The intent is to journal your thoughts as you engage with God and His Word. Don't be shy. Be you, be with God, and enjoy!

READ	OBSERVE	INTERPRET
¹In the beginning, God created the heavens and the earth. ²The earth was without form and void, and darkness was over the face of the deep. And the Spirit of God was hovering over the face of the waters. ³And God said, "Let there be light," and there was light. ⁴And God saw that the light was good. And God separated the light from the darkness. ⁵God called the light Day, and the darkness he called Night. And there was evening and there was morning, the first day.		

KEY WORDS	DEFINITIONS	CROSS REFERENCES

MAIN POINT(S)	APPLY

PRAY

sample *lesson*

GENESIS 1:1-5 | FOR THOSE CRAZY, BUSY DAYS

We're busy. Life can be hectic. Some days, you may not have time to go deep in your study. That's okay. One truth from God's Word transforms hearts which often transforms the day. Using Genesis 1:1-5, here's what a study might look like with very little time. The goal is to observe, interpret, and apply just *one* thing (particularly about who God is):

READ	OBSERVE	INTERPRET
¹In the beginning, God created the heavens and the earth. ²The earth was without form and void, and darkness was over the face of the deep. And the Spirit of God was hovering over the face of the waters. ³And God said, "Let there be light," and there was light. ⁴And God saw that the light was good. And God separated the light from the darkness. ⁵God called the light Day, and the darkness he called Night. And there was evening and there was morning, the first day.	The Who? What do I learn about Him?	God! He's mentioned 6 times. - God was in the beginning. - God created. - His Spirit hovered. - He speaks. And there is light. - He sees: the light is good. - He separates: the light from the darkness - He calls (names) the light and darkness: day and night.

KEY WORDS	DEFINITIONS	CROSS REFERENCES
void	empty (NIV translation)	

MAIN POINT(S)

In the beginning, God created the heavens and earth.

APPLY

God, who was in the beginning, creates. Hovers. Speaks light. Separates light from darkness.

He still does that today. Praise Him! Thank Him!

PRAY

Creator God, I praise You! You were there in the beginning, hovering over the waters. I wonder what You thought as You hovered over the emptiness. Thank You for Your Creation. It's beautiful. Amazing. LORD, You spoke light into the darkness in the beginning. Would You please do that today? Help me to hear You and listen. Lead me in Your Light.

sample *lesson*

GENESIS 1:1-5 | GOING DEEPER

Do you have time to linger in God's Word? Using Genesis 1:1-5, here's an example of what a more extensive study could look like. Observe as much or as little as you like.

Remember: No two journals will look the same. There's so much more to observe!

READ	OBSERVE	INTERPRET
¹ In the beginning, God created the heavens and the earth. ² The earth was without form and void, and darkness was over the face of the deep. And the Spirit of God was hovering over the face of the waters. ³ And God said, "Let there be light," and there was light. ⁴ And God saw that the light was good. And God separated the light from the darkness. ⁵ God called the light Day, and the darkness he called Night. And there was evening and there was morning, the first day.	The Who? What do I learn about Him? Earth- 2x Darkness- 3x Light- 5x When? God says, "Let there be light" and then it exists! Who else can do this?! What power is this?	God! He's mentioned 6 times. - God was in the beginning. - God created. - His Spirit hovered. - He speaks. And there is light. - He sees: the light is good. - He separates: the light from the darkness - He calls (names) the light and darkness: day and night. The beginning (when God created the heavens and the earth.) Light is significant. God saw it was good. Only God speaks and it is so. He is all powerful and almighty.

KEY WORDS	DEFINITIONS	CROSS REFERENCES
beginning	the point at which something begins, the start *(Webster's)*	**John 1:1-3** In the beginning was the Word, and the Word was with God, and the Word was God. He was in the beginning with God. All things were made through him, and without him was not any thing made that was made.
created	to bring into existence *(Bible dictionary)*	
void	empty *(NIV translation)*	**II Corinthians 4:6** For God, who said, "Let light shine out of darkness," has shone in our hearts to give the light of the knowledge of the glory of God in the face of Jesus Christ.
light	contrasted to darkness	
good	having desirable or positive qualities	

MAIN POINT(S)

In the beginning God created the heavens and the earth. He speaks light and there is light!

APPLY

Trust God. He was in the beginning. He creates beautiful things out of chaos and emptiness. He speaks light and it is so. He separates light from darkness. He still does that today. He can do this in my life and the lives of my loved ones. **Worship!** "Worthy are you, our LORD and God, to receive glory and honor and power, for you created all things, and by your will they existed and were created." *(Rev. 4:11)*

PRAY

God, You are worthy of glory and honor and power, for in the beginning you created all things, and by your will they exist and were created. Thank You. Thank You for life and light. And thank You for Jesus, the True Light, Who was with You in the beginning. Your Spirit hovered over the emptiness, the waste, the chaos, and then, You spoke light into the darkness! Thank You that Your Spirit continues to hover near. What a gift! Please speak Your light into my life and the lives of these dear ones. Help us to hear You and listen. Lead us in Your Light.

YOU DID IT! That's it. That's all there is to the SIMPLY BIBLE inductive process. If this is your first time, the process may feel a little awkward at first. Don't worry. You probably don't remember how clumsy and time-consuming it was the very first time you tried tying your shoe, riding a bike, or driving a car. Practice helps. The same will be true for Bible study. Like riding a bicycle, it gets easier.

Likewise, please know that your study guide will look different from most others. You are unique and special. And so, your observations and application will be unique. Every artist creates something different with her "blank page."

Indeed, you've probably gathered by now that this study is different. And different often falls outside our comfort zones. The purpose of this Bible study is that you may confidently read, understand, and apply God's Word like never before, using *simply the Bible*.

IT WILL REQUIRE A COMMITMENT. Would you please commit to finish this study book? By the end, with consistency, perseverance, and time spent with Him, you will better know God, His Word, and your identity in Him.

You're more observant, smarter, and stronger than you think you are. God created you that way. He desires to be known. He wants to show you that you are loved, valued, and never alone. Lean into Him. Ask, seek, and you will find. His grace is sufficient. His power is made perfect in our weakness.

> As the rain and the snow come down from heaven,
> and do not return to it without watering the earth
> and making it bud and flourish,
> so that it yields seed for the sower and bread for the eater,
>
> so is my word that goes out from my mouth:
> It will not return to me empty,
> but will accomplish what I desire
> and achieve the purpose for which I sent it.

> You will go out in joy and be led forth in peace;
> the mountains and hills will burst into song before you,
> and all the trees of the field will clap their hands.
>
> ISAIAH 55:10-12

LORD God Almighty, Thank You for Your Word! Like rain and snow watering the earth so that it might bud and flourish, may Your Word now water our hearts, minds, and souls, that our love for You and for one another would bud and flourish. May Your purposes and desires be accomplished. As we study with You, may we go out in joy and be led forth in Your peace. With all creation may we sing and clap for joy and bring glory to Your Name…

ABOVE ALL YOU SHALL KEEP MY SABBATHS, FOR THIS IS A SIGN BETWEEN ME AND YOU THROUGHOUT YOUR GENERATIONS, THAT YOU MAY KNOW THAT I, THE LORD, SANCTIFY YOU.

EXODUS 31:13

in *context*

EXAMINING THE CONTEXT OF **EXODUS**

in *context*

EXAMINING THE CONTEXT OF EXODUS

Within the 66 books of the Bible's Old and New Testaments, Exodus is located as the second Old Testament book. It is part of what is known as the Pentateuch, or the first five books of the Bible: Genesis, Exodus, Leviticus, Numbers and Deuteronomy. Jewish tradition refers to this as the Torah, and it is known as the Law throughout the Scriptures. [1]

Authorship of all five books, including Exodus, is attributed to Moses within both Jewish and Christian tradition. Some Biblical scholars view Exodus as a product of a later author or editor. However, if this were to be true, most agree that the influence is limited. [2] There is no denying that Moses is the primary source of this written document, which provides eye-witness accounts of Israel's exodus from Egypt. [3]

In some ways, the first part of Exodus offers biographical details of Moses himself, his birth, and the beginning of his ministry. Yet the main purpose of Exodus is not to deify Moses, but to record the story of God's deliverance and fulfilled promises through this nation of Israel, ultimately displaying God's redemptive power and bringing glory to His Name.

Exodus begins with a recap of how the people of Israel ended up in Egypt, which directly ties into the ending of Genesis. However, dating the events of Exodus have been

---

[1] T. Desmond Alexander. *From Paradise to the Promised Land: An Introduction to the Pentateuch* (Grand Rapids, MI: Baker Books, 2012), 3.

[2] Andrew E. Hill and John H. Walton. *A Survey of the Old Testament* (Grand Rapids, MI: Zondervan, 2009), 103.

[3] Bruce Wilkinson and Kenneth Boa. *Walk Thru The Bible* (Nashville, Tennessee: Thomas Nelson Publishers, 1983), 13.

problematic for scholars. Ideas abound, but two basic positions are promoted: an early or a later dating. The early dating identifies Thutmose III as the oppressing pharaoh and Amenophis II (1450-1425 BC) as the pharaoh of the exodus. A later dating identifies Rameses I and Seti I as the oppressing pharaohs with Rameses II as the pharaoh (1304-1237BC) of the exodus. [1]

Whether considering the early or later dating, each Pharaoh mentioned reigned in the New Kingdom era of Egyptian history or the Late Bronze to Early Iron age of ancient Near East history. Notably, the author of Exodus was not concerned with identifying the specific Egyptian king. Rather, Moses highlights the Hero of the story as the LORD Himself.

Pharoah, being the supreme ruler over all the people of Egypt, made the laws, owned all the land, collected taxes, and oversaw wars. Yet Pharaoh also bore a very priestly role. The Egyptian culture centered around an expansive Egyptian pantheon numbering more then 2000 gods.

Pharaoh himself was revered as a god who would mediate between these many gods and the people. In this intercessory role, he possessed oversight of religious ceremonies and built temples to honor the gods that established his rule on earth. [2] A pretty powerful gig.

For our study, it is necessary to keep in mind Pharoah's responsibility: he was to intercede between the gods and the people. Understanding a bit of Egyptian culture will help us to see the book of Exodus through an Ancient Near East lens.

Putting this altogether, here are three simplified rules for studying Old Testament Biblical narrative:

---

[1] Andrew E. Hill and John H. Walton. *A Survey of the Old Testament* (Grand Rapids, MI: Zondervan, 2009), 103.

[2] **Pharaoh**. *World History Encyclopedia*. World History Publishing, Inc. https://www.worldhistory.org/pharaoh/ (accessed: Feb. 2023).

(1) God is always the hero. One might be tempted to view Moses or others as the hero of the Exodus story. And although Moses plays a significant role, he is not the hero. Likewise, it is common to make Scripture about ourselves. Yes, the narrative is here for our benefit, but it is not *about* us. The stories are about God and the characters in the story. The hero will always be God. To keep Him in His rightful place, it is helpful to ask, "What does this passage tell me about God?"

(2) Read literally. We don't want to read anything into the text that is not there. So read literally. The author is telling a story. He is providing a historical account of real people and real events. There are no symbols. No allegories. No hidden meanings. Learn directly from God's work through true stories about real people.

(3) Look for the spiritual lesson. These are real people. Like us, they are fallible and finite. What does that mean? They make mistakes. They die. Relate with them. Seek to identify with them, remembering that they are former slaves. Walk in their shoes. Ask, "What did they feel? What did they endure? What did they do right? What did they do wrong?" It is okay to learn by comparing our lives to theirs. Whether good or bad, we can learn from others. Let's not make their same mistakes. And if they were faithful, let's follow in their footsteps. Find the spiritual lessons and learn a principal for living and walking with God. That's our goal! Walking with God.

draw a *map*

USE THE SPACE BELOW TO DRAW A MAP OF ANCIENT ISRAEL, FOR YOUR OWN REFERENCE THROUGHOUT THE STUDY OF EXODUS

the ten *commandments*

WRITE OUT THE TEN COMMANDMENTS. *(SEE EXODUS 20)*

1
2
3
4
5
6
7
8
9
10

What do you learn about God and His heart from studying the ten commandments?

draw a *diagram*

USE THE SPACE BELOW TO DRAW A DIAGRAM OF THE TABERNACLE, FOR YOUR OWN REFERENCE THROUGHOUT THE STUDY OF EXODUS

BUT THE LORD SAID TO MOSES, "WHOEVER HAS SINNED AGAINST ME, I WILL BLOT OUT OF MY BOOK."

EXODUS 32:33

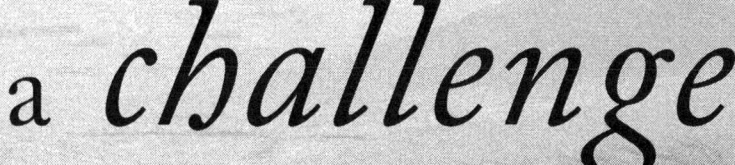

a *challenge*

KNOW & ENJOY THE GOD OF THE OLD TESTAMENT

AND ALL THE PEOPLE ANSWERED WITH ONE VOICE AND SAID, "ALL THE WORDS THAT THE LORD HAS SPOKEN WE WILL DO."

EXODUS 24:3

a *challenge*
KNOW & ENJOY THE GOD OF THE OLD TESTAMENT

Whenever we study Old Testament narrative, God stands as the Hero of the story. This is certainly true for the narrative of Exodus that clearly exhibits the heart and character of God. Yet, one problem we encounter when studying Scripture is that we bring with us our presuppositions and assumptions about God and the Bible. That's a fancy way of saying that we bring with us a host of things we already *think* we know about God and His Word.

We bring our belief or lack of belief. We bring our family histories, church experiences, and traditions. We bring our personality bents and political biases and so much more. These are not necessarily good or bad within themselves. The problem is: assumptions cloud our vision. It's as if we have blinders on that keep us from seeing the passage in black and white that sits directly before our eyes. Rather, our goal is to read God's Word afresh, as if we have never read it before. In this way, we can know and enjoy God for Who He really is.

That's the goal of this challenge: to enable us to let go of any baggage that we carry with us about the God of the Old Testament. This challenge is purposefully designed to help us know and understand the God of Exodus as if we are getting to know Him for the first time. In the process, may we enjoy Him, be connected to Him, have our hearts transformed by Him, and be more like Him.

For each book of the Exodus series, we will be challenged to **ponder** Exodus 34:6-7. In these two verses, God introduces Himself. In essence, He writes His own bio. When we meditate on this passage, we meditate on Who God is. Utilizing the SIMPLY BIBLE format, listen and soak in His goodness. Know and enjoy God.

a *challenge*

EXODUS 34:6-7

READ	OBSERVE	INTERPRET
⁶ The LORD passed before him and proclaimed, "The LORD, the LORD, a God merciful and gracious, slow to anger, and abounding in steadfast love and faithfulness, ⁷ keeping steadfast love for thousands, forgiving iniquity and transgression and sin, but who will by no means clear the guilty, visiting the iniquity of the fathers on the children and the children's children, to the third and the fourth generation."		

KEY WORDS	DEFINITIONS	CROSS REFERENCES

MAIN POINT(S)	APPLY

PRAY

chapter *one*

EXODUS 24

take *note*

EXODUS 24

take *note*
EXODUS 24

day *one*

EXODUS 24:1-2

READ	OBSERVE	INTERPRET
¹ Then he said to Moses, "Come up to the Lord, you and Aaron, Nadab, and Abihu, and seventy of the elders of Israel, and worship from afar. ² Moses alone shall come near to the Lord, but the others shall not come near, and the people shall not come up with him."		

KEY WORDS	DEFINITIONS	CROSS REFERENCES

MAIN POINT(S)	APPLY

PRAY

day *two*

EXODUS 24:3-8

READ

³ Moses came and told the people all the words of the Lord and all the rules. And all the people answered with one voice and said, "All the words that the Lord has spoken we will do." ⁴ And Moses wrote down all the words of the Lord. He rose early in the morning and built an altar at the foot of the mountain, and twelve pillars, according to the twelve tribes of Israel. ⁵ And he sent young men of the people of Israel, who offered burnt offerings and sacrificed peace offerings of oxen to the Lord. ⁶ And Moses took half of the blood and put it in basins, and half of the blood he threw against the altar. ⁷ Then he took the Book of the Covenant and read it in the hearing of the people. And they said, "All that the Lord has spoken we will do, and we will be obedient." ⁸ And Moses took the blood and threw it on the people and said, "Behold the blood of the covenant that the Lord has made with you in accordance with all these words."

OBSERVE

INTERPRET

| KEY WORDS | DEFINITIONS | CROSS REFERENCES |

| MAIN POINT(S) | APPLY |

PRAY

day *three*

EXODUS 24:9-11

READ	OBSERVE	INTERPRET
⁹ Then Moses and Aaron, Nadab, and Abihu, and seventy of the elders of Israel went up, ¹⁰ and they saw the God of Israel. There was under his feet as it were a pavement of sapphire stone, like the very heaven for clearness. ¹¹ And he did not lay his hand on the chief men of the people of Israel; they beheld God, and ate and drank.		

KEY WORDS	DEFINITIONS	CROSS REFERENCES

MAIN POINT(S)	APPLY

PRAY

day *four*

EXODUS 24:12-18

READ

¹² The Lord said to Moses, "Come up to me on the mountain and wait there, that I may give you the tablets of stone, with the law and the commandment, which I have written for their instruction." ¹³ So Moses rose with his assistant Joshua, and Moses went up into the mountain of God. ¹⁴ And he said to the elders, "Wait here for us until we return to you. And behold, Aaron and Hur are with you. Whoever has a dispute, let him go to them."

¹⁵ Then Moses went up on the mountain, and the cloud covered the mountain. ¹⁶ The glory of the Lord dwelt on Mount Sinai, and the cloud covered it six days. And on the seventh day he called to Moses out of the midst of the cloud. ¹⁷ Now the appearance of the glory of the Lord was like a devouring fire on the top of the mountain in the sight of the people of Israel. ¹⁸ Moses entered the cloud and went up on the mountain. And Moses was on the mountain forty days and forty nights.

OBSERVE

INTERPRET

KEY WORDS	DEFINITIONS	CROSS REFERENCES

MAIN POINT(S)	APPLY

PRAY

day *five*

EXODUS 24 | REVIEW & DISCUSSION QUESTIONS

1 Summary:	2 Write out your favorite verse from the passage, perhaps in your own words:
3 Define *worship*.	4 Describe the spectrum of locations assigned for worship (24:1-2). Who can draw near? Where are the people? How will this mirror the tabernacle?
5 Who can draw near to God today? Explain. (See Luke 15:1 and John 4:23-24.)	6 Define *covenant*. What agreement do the Israelites make with God? (24:3, 24:7)

7 What has God promised the Israelites? (See Exodus 19:5-6.)

8 Throwing blood at people is difficult for our 21st century sensibilities to comprehend. Explain the significance.

9 How do the Israelite leaders experience God? Why might the author mention eating and drinking? (24:9-11)

10 For what purpose does God call Moses up the mountain? How would you describe the role of Moses? What is God's role?

11 How would you define or explain *the glory of the Lord*? How is the glory of the Lord manifested to the Israelites?

12 What do you learn about God from this chapter?

take it to *heart*

USE THIS SPACE TO WRITE OUT OR JOURNAL A FAVORITE VERSE OR PASSAGE FROM THIS WEEK'S STUDY

chapter *two*

EXODUS 25 & 26

take *note*

NOTES ON EXODUS 25 & 26

take *note*

NOTES ON EXODUS 25 & 26

day *one*

EXODUS 25:1-22

READ

[1] The Lord said to Moses, [2] "Speak to the people of Israel, that they take for me a contribution. From every man whose heart moves him you shall receive the contribution for me. [3] And this is the contribution that you shall receive from them: gold, silver, and bronze, [4] blue and purple and scarlet yarns and fine twined linen, goats' hair, [5] tanned rams' skins, goatskins, acacia wood, [6] oil for the lamps, spices for the anointing oil and for the fragrant incense, [7] onyx stones, and stones for setting, for the ephod and for the breastpiece. [8] And let them make me a sanctuary, that I may dwell in their midst. [9] Exactly as I show you concerning the pattern of the tabernacle, and of all its furniture, so you shall make it.

[10] "They shall make an ark of acacia wood. Two cubits and a half shall be its length, a cubit and a half its breadth, and a cubit and a half its height. [11] You shall overlay it with pure gold, inside and outside shall you overlay it, and you shall make on it a molding of gold around it. [12] You shall cast four rings of gold for it and put them on its four feet, two rings on the one side of it, and two rings on the other side of it. [13] You shall make poles of acacia wood and overlay them with gold. [14] And you shall put the poles into the rings on the sides of the ark to carry the ark by them. [15] The poles shall remain in the rings of the ark; they shall not be taken from it. [16] And you shall put into the ark the testimony that I shall give you.

[17] "You shall make a mercy seat of pure gold. Two cubits and a half shall be its length, and a cubit and a half its breadth. [18] And you shall make two cherubim of gold; of hammered work shall you make them, on the two ends of the mercy seat. [19] Make one cherub on the one end, and one cherub on the other end. Of one piece with the mercy seat shall you make the cherubim on its two ends. [20] The cherubim shall spread out their wings above, overshadowing the mercy seat with their wings, their faces one to another; toward the mercy seat shall the faces of the cherubim be. [21] And you shall put the mercy seat on the top of the ark, and in the ark you shall put the testimony that I shall give you. [22] There I will meet with you, and from above the mercy seat, from between the two cherubim that are on the ark of the testimony, I will speak with you about all that I will give you in commandment for the people of Israel.

OBSERVE	INTERPRET

KEY WORDS	DEFINITIONS	CROSS REFERENCES

MAIN POINT(S)	APPLY

PRAY

day *two*

EXODUS 25:23-40

READ

23 "You shall make a table of acacia wood. Two cubits shall be its length, a cubit its breadth, and a cubit and a half its height. 24 You shall overlay it with pure gold and make a molding of gold around it. 25 And you shall make a rim around it a handbreadth wide, and a molding of gold around the rim. 26 And you shall make for it four rings of gold, and fasten the rings to the four corners at its four legs. 27 Close to the frame the rings shall lie, as holders for the poles to carry the table. 28 You shall make the poles of acacia wood, and overlay them with gold, and the table shall be carried with these. 29 And you shall make its plates and dishes for incense, and its flagons and bowls with which to pour drink offerings; you shall make them of pure gold. 30 And you shall set the bread of the Presence on the table before me regularly.

31 "You shall make a lampstand of pure gold. The lampstand shall be made of hammered work: its base, its stem, its cups, its calyxes, and its flowers shall be of one piece with it. 32 And there shall be six branches going out of its sides, three branches of the lampstand out of one side of it and three branches of the lampstand out of the other side of it; 33 three cups made like almond blossoms, each with calyx and flower, on one branch, and three cups made like almond blossoms, each with calyx and flower, on the other branch—so for the six branches going out of the lampstand. 34 And on the lampstand itself there shall be four cups made like almond blossoms, with their calyxes and flowers, 35 and a calyx of one piece with it under each pair of the six branches going out from the lampstand. 36 Their calyxes and their branches shall be of one piece with it, the whole of it a single piece of hammered work of pure gold. 37 You shall make seven lamps for it. And the lamps shall be set up so as to give light on the space in front of it. 38 Its tongs and their trays shall be of pure gold. 39 It shall be made, with all these utensils, out of a talent of pure gold. 40 And see that you make them after the pattern for them, which is being shown you on the mountain.

	OBSERVE	INTERPRET

KEY WORDS	DEFINITIONS	CROSS REFERENCES

MAIN POINT(S)	APPLY

PRAY

day *three*

EXODUS 26:1-14

READ

¹ "Moreover, you shall make the tabernacle with ten curtains of fine twined linen and blue and purple and scarlet yarns; you shall make them with cherubim skillfully worked into them. ² The length of each curtain shall be twenty-eight cubits, and the breadth of each curtain four cubits; all the curtains shall be the same size. ³ Five curtains shall be coupled to one another, and the other five curtains shall be coupled to one another. ⁴ And you shall make loops of blue on the edge of the outermost curtain in the first set. Likewise you shall make loops on the edge of the outermost curtain in the second set. ⁵ Fifty loops you shall make on the one curtain, and fifty loops you shall make on the edge of the curtain that is in the second set; the loops shall be opposite one another. ⁶ And you shall make fifty clasps of gold, and couple the curtains one to the other with the clasps, so that the tabernacle may be a single whole.

⁷ "You shall also make curtains of goats' hair for a tent over the tabernacle; eleven curtains shall you make. ⁸ The length of each curtain shall be thirty cubits, and the breadth of each curtain four cubits. The eleven curtains shall be the same size. ⁹ You shall couple five curtains by themselves, and six curtains by themselves, and the sixth curtain you shall double over at the front of the tent. ¹⁰ You shall make fifty loops on the edge of the curtain that is outermost in one set, and fifty loops on the edge of the curtain that is outermost in the second set.

¹¹ "You shall make fifty clasps of bronze, and put the clasps into the loops, and couple the tent together that it may be a single whole. ¹² And the part that remains of the curtains of the tent, the half curtain that remains, shall hang over the back of the tabernacle. ¹³ And the extra that remains in the length of the curtains, the cubit on the one side, and the cubit on the other side, shall hang over the sides of the tabernacle, on this side and that side, to cover it. ¹⁴ And you shall make for the tent a covering of tanned rams' skins and a covering of goatskins on top.

OBSERVE	INTERPRET

KEY WORDS	DEFINITIONS	CROSS REFERENCES

MAIN POINT(S)	APPLY

PRAY

day *four*

EXODUS 26:15-37

READ

¹⁵ "You shall make upright frames for the tabernacle of acacia wood. ¹⁶ Ten cubits shall be the length of a frame, and a cubit and a half the breadth of each frame. ¹⁷ There shall be two tenons in each frame, for fitting together. So shall you do for all the frames of the tabernacle. ¹⁸ You shall make the frames for the tabernacle: twenty frames for the south side; ¹⁹ and forty bases of silver you shall make under the twenty frames, two bases under one frame for its two tenons, and two bases under the next frame for its two tenons; ²⁰ and for the second side of the tabernacle, on the north side twenty frames, ²¹ and their forty bases of silver, two bases under one frame, and two bases under the next frame. ²² And for the rear of the tabernacle westward you shall make six frames. ²³ And you shall make two frames for corners of the tabernacle in the rear; ²⁴ they shall be separate beneath, but joined at the top, at the first ring. Thus shall it be with both of them; they shall form the two corners. ²⁵ And there shall be eight frames, with their bases of silver, sixteen bases; two bases under one frame, and two bases under another frame.

²⁶ "You shall make bars of acacia wood, five for the frames of the one side of the tabernacle, ²⁷ and five bars for the frames of the other side of the tabernacle, and five bars for the frames of the side of the tabernacle at the rear westward. ²⁸ The middle bar, halfway up the frames, shall run from end to end. ²⁹ You shall overlay the frames with gold and shall make their rings of gold for holders for the bars, and you shall overlay the bars with gold. ³⁰ Then you shall erect the tabernacle according to the plan for it that you were shown on the mountain.

³¹ "And you shall make a veil of blue and purple and scarlet yarns and fine twined linen. It shall be made with cherubim skillfully worked into it. ³² And you shall hang it on four pillars of acacia overlaid with gold, with hooks of gold, on four bases of silver. ³³ And you shall hang the veil from the clasps, and bring the ark of the testimony in there within the veil. And the veil shall separate for you the Holy Place from the Most Holy. ³⁴ You shall put the mercy seat on the ark of the testimony in the Most Holy Place. ³⁵ And you shall set the table outside the veil, and the lampstand on the south side of the tabernacle opposite the table, and you shall put the table on the north side.

	OBSERVE	INTERPRET
³⁶ "You shall make a screen for the entrance of the tent, of blue and purple and scarlet yarns and fine twined linen, embroidered with needlework. ³⁷ And you shall make for the screen five pillars of acacia, and overlay them with gold. Their hooks shall be of gold, and you shall cast five bases of bronze for them.		

KEY WORDS	DEFINITIONS	CROSS REFERENCES

MAIN POINT(S)	APPLY

PRAY

day *five*

EXODUS 25 & 26 | REVIEW & DISCUSSION QUESTIONS

1 Summary:	2 Write out your favorite verse from the passage, perhaps in your own words:
3 Define *contribution*. Who is to give and why? Are the people under compulsion to give? What does this tell you about God's heart?	4 What is the purpose of a sanctuary? Tabernacle? (See Exodus 25:8, 25:22, and Hebrews 8:5)
5 Define *pattern*. Who is the master designer and how is the sanctuary to be made? (25:9)	6 What is the ark of the covenant? Explain its purpose.

7 What practical purpose does the mercy seat serve? What does it symbolize? (See Exodus 25:22 and Leviticus 16:2.)

8 Describe the table for bread. What does bread symbolize? (See John 6:48.)

9 How many lamps are on the lampstand? What might the lampstand prefigure?

10 Exodus 26 goes into great detail about the tabernacle itself. What is the purpose of the curtains? How does the tabernacle point to Christ? (See Mark 15:37-38.)

11 Consider how we worship today by reading Hebrews 9:7-14 and 10:20. How does this touch your heart?

12 Ponder the intricate instructions for the tabernacle. Worship God for the things you learned about Him in this chapter.

take it to *heart*

USE THIS SPACE TO WRITE OUT OR JOURNAL A FAVORITE VERSE OR PASSAGE FROM THIS WEEK'S STUDY

> YOU SHALL MAKE HOLY GARMENTS FOR AARON YOUR BROTHER, FOR GLORY AND FOR BEAUTY.
>
> EXODUS 28:2

chapter *three*

EXODUS 27 & 28

take *note*

NOTES ON EXODUS 27 & 28

take *note*

NOTES ON EXODUS 27 & 28

day *one*

EXODUS 27:1-8

READ

¹ "You shall make the altar of acacia wood, five cubits long and five cubits broad. The altar shall be square, and its height shall be three cubits. ² <u>And you shall make horns for it on its four corners;</u> its horns shall be of one piece with it, and you shall overlay it with bronze. ³ You shall make pots for it to receive its ashes, and shovels and basins and forks and fire pans. You shall make all its utensils of bronze. ⁴ You shall also make for it a grating, a network of bronze, and on the net you shall make four bronze rings at its four corners. ⁵ And you shall set it under the ledge of the altar so that the net extends halfway down the altar. ⁶ And you shall make poles for the altar, poles of acacia wood, and overlay them with bronze. ⁷ And the poles shall be put through the rings, so that the poles are on the two sides of the altar when it is carried. ⁸ You shall make it hollow, with boards. As it has been shown you on the mountain, so shall it be made.

OBSERVE

INTERPRET

KEY WORDS	DEFINITIONS	CROSS REFERENCES
Altar →	→ "God's table" a raised place for worship + sacrifice, where people honor God with offerings.	1 Kings 1:50-53 (goes w/ Ex. 27:2) Grasping the horns of the altar was a means of seeking general asylum. The hope was that he would be seen as belonging to God & thus under protection.

MAIN POINT(S)

APPLY

PRAY

day *two*

EXODUS 27:9-21

READ

⁹ "You shall make the court of the tabernacle. On the south side the court shall have hangings of fine twined linen a hundred cubits long for one side. ¹⁰ Its twenty pillars and their twenty bases shall be of bronze, but the hooks of the pillars and their fillets shall be of silver. ¹¹ And likewise for its length on the north side there shall be hangings a hundred cubits long, its pillars twenty and their bases twenty, of bronze, but the hooks of the pillars and their fillets shall be of silver. ¹² And for the breadth of the court on the west side there shall be hangings for fifty cubits, with ten pillars and ten bases. ¹³ The breadth of the court on the front to the east shall be fifty cubits. ¹⁴ The hangings for the one side of the gate shall be fifteen cubits, with their three pillars and three bases. ¹⁵ On the other side the hangings shall be fifteen cubits, with their three pillars and three bases. ¹⁶ For the gate of the court there shall be a screen twenty cubits long, of <u>blue and purple and scarlet yarns</u> and fine twined linen, embroidered with needlework. It shall have four pillars and with them four bases. ¹⁷ All the pillars around the court shall be filleted with silver. Their hooks shall be of silver, and their bases of bronze. ¹⁸ The length of the court shall be a hundred cubits, the breadth fifty, and the height five cubits, with hangings of fine twined linen and bases of bronze. ¹⁹ All the utensils of the tabernacle for every use, and all its pegs and all the pegs of the court, shall be of bronze.

²⁰ "You shall command the people of Israel that they bring to you pure beaten olive oil for the light, that <u>a lamp may regularly be set up to burn</u>. ²¹ In the tent of meeting, outside the veil that is before the testimony, Aaron and his sons shall tend it from evening to morning before the Lord. It shall be a statute forever to be observed throughout their generations by the people of Israel.

	OBSERVE	INTERPRET
	screen/veil → blue, purple & scarlet yarns "a lamp may regularly be set up to burn" priesthood of Aaron set up to continue priestly duties (tending the lamp)	- blue -- divine; sacred. - purple -- royalty; transformation - scarlet -- blood of Christ; atonement. * Items outside the tabernacle itself were made with silver & bronze, which were less costly than gold.

KEY WORDS	DEFINITIONS	CROSS REFERENCES

MAIN POINT(S)	APPLY

PRAY

IT SHALL BE A STATUTE
FOREVER TO BE OBSERVED
THROUGHOUT THEIR GENERATIONS
BY THE PEOPLE OF ISRAEL.

EXODUS 27:21

day *three*

EXODUS 28:1-21

> ### READ
>
> [1] "Then bring near to you Aaron your brother, and his sons with him, from among the people of Israel, to serve me as priests—Aaron and Aaron's sons, Nadab and Abihu, Eleazar and Ithamar. [2] And you shall make holy garments for Aaron your brother, for glory and for beauty. [3] You shall speak to all the skillful, whom I have filled with a spirit of skill, that they make Aaron's garments to consecrate him for my priesthood. [4] These are the garments that they shall make: a breastpiece, an ephod, a robe, a coat of checker work, a turban, and a sash. They shall make holy garments for Aaron your brother and his sons to serve me as priests. [5] They shall receive gold, blue and purple and scarlet yarns, and fine twined linen.
>
> [6] "And they shall make the ephod of gold, of blue and purple and scarlet yarns, and of fine twined linen, skillfully worked. [7] It shall have two shoulder pieces attached to its two edges, so that it may be joined together. [8] And the skillfully woven band on it shall be made like it and be of one piece with it, of gold, blue and purple and scarlet yarns, and fine twined linen. [9] You shall take two onyx stones, and engrave on them the names of the sons of Israel, [10] six of their names on the one stone, and the names of the remaining six on the other stone, in the order of their birth. [11] As a jeweler engraves signets, so shall you engrave the two stones with the names of the sons of Israel. You shall enclose them in settings of gold filigree. [12] And you shall set the two stones on the shoulder pieces of the ephod, as stones of remembrance for the sons of Israel. And Aaron shall bear their names before the Lord on his two shoulders for remembrance. [13] You shall make settings of gold filigree, [14] and two chains of pure gold, twisted like cords; and you shall attach the corded chains to the settings.
>
> [15] "You shall make a breastpiece of judgment, in skilled work. In the style of the ephod you shall make it—of gold, blue and purple and scarlet yarns, and fine twined linen shall you make it. [16] It shall be square and doubled, a span its length and a span its breadth. [17] You shall set in it four rows of stones. A row of sardius, topaz, and carbuncle shall be the first row; [18] and the second row an emerald, a sapphire, and a diamond; [19] and the third row a jacinth, an agate, and an amethyst; [20] and the fourth row a beryl, an onyx, and a jasper. They shall be set in gold filigree. [21] There shall be twelve stones with their names according to the names of the sons of Israel. They shall be like signets, each engraved with its name, for the twelve tribes.

OBSERVE	INTERPRET

| KEY WORDS | DEFINITIONS | CROSS REFERENCES |

| MAIN POINT(S) | APPLY |

PRAY

day *four*

EXODUS 28:22-42

READ

²² You shall make for the breastpiece twisted chains like cords, of pure gold. ²³ And you shall make for the breastpiece two rings of gold, and put the two rings on the two edges of the breastpiece. ²⁴ And you shall put the two cords of gold in the two rings at the edges of the breastpiece. ²⁵ The two ends of the two cords you shall attach to the two settings of filigree, and so attach it in front to the shoulder pieces of the ephod. ²⁶ You shall make two rings of gold, and put them at the two ends of the breastpiece, on its inside edge next to the ephod. ²⁷ And you shall make two rings of gold, and attach them in front to the lower part of the two shoulder pieces of the ephod, at its seam above the skillfully woven band of the ephod. ²⁸ And they shall bind the breastpiece by its rings to the rings of the ephod with a lace of blue, so that it may lie on the skillfully woven band of the ephod, so that the breastpiece shall not come loose from the ephod. ²⁹ So Aaron shall bear the names of the sons of Israel in the breastpiece of judgment on his heart, when he goes into the Holy Place, to bring them to regular remembrance before the Lord. ³⁰ And in the breastpiece of judgment you shall put the Urim and the Thummim, and they shall be on Aaron's heart, when he goes in before the Lord. Thus Aaron shall bear the judgment of the people of Israel on his heart before the Lord regularly.

³¹ "You shall make the robe of the ephod all of blue. ³² It shall have an opening for the head in the middle of it, with a woven binding around the opening, like the opening in a garment, so that it may not tear. ³³ On its hem you shall make pomegranates of blue and purple and scarlet yarns, around its hem, with bells of gold between them, ³⁴ a golden bell and a pomegranate, a golden bell and a pomegranate, around the hem of the robe. ³⁵ And it shall be on Aaron when he ministers, and its sound shall be heard when he goes into the Holy Place before the Lord, and when he comes out, so that he does not die.

³⁶ "You shall make a plate of pure gold and engrave on it, like the engraving of a signet, 'Holy to the Lord.' ³⁷ And you shall fasten it on the turban by a cord of blue. It shall be on the front of the turban. ³⁸ It shall be on Aaron's forehead, and Aaron shall bear any guilt from the holy things that the people of Israel consecrate as their holy gifts. It shall regularly be on his forehead, that they may be accepted before the Lord.

	OBSERVE	INTERPRET
³⁹ "You shall weave the coat in checker work of fine linen, and you shall make a turban of fine linen, and you shall make a sash embroidered with needlework. ⁴⁰ "For Aaron's sons you shall make coats and sashes and caps. You shall make them for glory and beauty. ⁴¹ And you shall put them on Aaron your brother, and on his sons with him, and shall anoint them and ordain them and consecrate them, that they may serve me as priests. ⁴² You shall make for them linen undergarments to cover their naked flesh. They shall reach from the hips to the thighs; ⁴³ and they shall be on Aaron and on his sons when they go into the tent of meeting or when they come near the altar to minister in the Holy Place, lest they bear guilt and die. This shall be a statute forever for him and for his offspring after him.		

KEY WORDS	DEFINITIONS	CROSS REFERENCES

MAIN POINT(S)	APPLY

PRAY

day *five*

EXODUS 27 & 28 | REVIEW & DISCUSSION QUESTIONS

1 Summary:	2 Write out your favorite verse from the passage, perhaps in your own words:
3 What is the purpose of the altar? (See Exodus 38:1.) Explain how our worship of God differs today. What sacrifices ought we offer to God? (See Hebrews 13:10-17.)	4 Notice the direction the tabernacle faces. In view of all of Scripture, why might this have significance?
5 Who will supply the oil for the lamp? Who is to maintain the lamp?	6 Who appoints Aaron and his sons to be priests? (See Exodus 28:1 and Hebrews 5:4.) Define the role of a priest. How does Aaron prefigure Christ? (See Hebrews 5:5, 7:26, and 9:11.)

7 What is the purpose of the special garments worn by Aaron and his sons?

8 Describe and explain the purpose of the two shoulder pieces.

9 Describe and explain the purpose of the breastplate of the ephod.

10 Describe Aaron's turban and its purpose.

11 What does the beauty of Aaron's garments tell you about God's heart and worship? Apply.

12 Worship God for the things you learned about Him in this chapter.

take it to *heart*

USE THIS SPACE TO WRITE OUT OR JOURNAL A FAVORITE VERSE OR PASSAGE FROM THIS WEEK'S STUDY

IT IS A PLEASING AROMA,
A FOOD OFFERING
TO THE LORD.

EXODUS 29:18

chapter *four*

EXODUS 29 & 30

take *note*

NOTES ON EXODUS 29 & 30

take *note*

NOTES ON EXODUS 29 & 30

day *one*

EXODUS 29:1-25

> READ
>
> ¹ "Now this is what you shall do to them to consecrate them, that they may serve me as priests. Take one bull of the herd and two rams without blemish, ² and unleavened bread, unleavened cakes mixed with oil, and unleavened wafers smeared with oil. You shall make them of fine wheat flour. ³ You shall put them in one basket and bring them in the basket, and bring the bull and the two rams. ⁴ You shall bring Aaron and his sons to the entrance of the tent of meeting and wash them with water. ⁵ Then you shall take the garments, and put on Aaron the coat and the robe of the ephod, and the ephod, and the breastpiece, and gird him with the skillfully woven band of the ephod. ⁶ And you shall set the turban on his head and put the holy crown on the turban. ⁷ You shall take the anointing oil and pour it on his head and anoint him. ⁸ Then you shall bring his sons and put coats on them, ⁹ and you shall gird Aaron and his sons with sashes and bind caps on them. And the priesthood shall be theirs by a statute forever. Thus you shall ordain Aaron and his sons.
>
> ¹⁰ "Then you shall bring the bull before the tent of meeting. Aaron and his sons shall lay their hands on the head of the bull. ¹¹ Then you shall kill the bull before the Lord at the entrance of the tent of meeting, ¹² and shall take part of the blood of the bull and put it on the horns of the altar with your finger, and the rest of the blood you shall pour out at the base of the altar. ¹³ And you shall take all the fat that covers the entrails, and the long lobe of the liver, and the two kidneys with the fat that is on them, and burn them on the altar. ¹⁴ But the flesh of the bull and its skin and its dung you shall burn with fire outside the camp; it is a sin offering.
>
> ¹⁵ "Then you shall take one of the rams, and Aaron and his sons shall lay their hands on the head of the ram, ¹⁶ and you shall kill the ram and shall take its blood and throw it against the sides of the altar. ¹⁷ Then you shall cut the ram into pieces, and wash its entrails and its legs, and put them with its pieces and its head, ¹⁸ and burn the whole ram on the altar. It is a burnt offering to the Lord. It is a pleasing aroma, a food offering to the Lord.
>
> ¹⁹ "You shall take the other ram, and Aaron and his sons shall lay their hands on the head of the ram, ²⁰ and you shall kill the ram and take part of its blood and put it on the tip of the right ear of Aaron and on the tips of the right ears of his sons, and on the thumbs of their right hands and on the great toes of their right feet, and throw the rest of the blood against

the sides of the altar. ²¹ Then you shall take part of the blood that is on the altar, and of the anointing oil, and sprinkle it on Aaron and his garments, and on his sons and his sons' garments with him. He and his garments shall be holy, and his sons and his sons' garments with him.

²² "You shall also take the fat from the ram and the fat tail and the fat that covers the entrails, and the long lobe of the liver and the two kidneys with the fat that is on them, and the right thigh (for it is a ram of ordination), ²³ and one loaf of bread and one cake of bread made with oil, and one wafer out of the basket of unleavened bread that is before the Lord. ²⁴ You shall put all these on the palms of Aaron and on the palms of his sons, and wave them for a wave offering before the Lord. ²⁵ Then you shall take them from their hands and burn them on the altar on top of the burnt offering, as a pleasing aroma before the Lord. It is a food offering to the Lord.

OBSERVE	INTERPRET

KEY WORDS	DEFINITIONS	CROSS REFERENCES

MAIN POINT(S)	APPLY

PRAY

day *two*

EXODUS 29:26-46

> ### READ
>
> ²⁶ "You shall take the breast of the ram of Aaron's ordination and wave it for a wave offering before the Lord, and it shall be your portion. ²⁷ And you shall consecrate the breast of the wave offering that is waved and the thigh of the priests' portion that is contributed from the ram of ordination, from what was Aaron's and his sons'. ²⁸ It shall be for Aaron and his sons as a perpetual due from the people of Israel, for it is a contribution. It shall be a contribution from the people of Israel from their peace offerings, their contribution to the Lord.
>
> ²⁹ "The holy garments of Aaron shall be for his sons after him; they shall be anointed in them and ordained in them. ³⁰ The son who succeeds him as priest, who comes into the tent of meeting to minister in the Holy Place, shall wear them seven days.
>
> ³¹ "You shall take the ram of ordination and boil its flesh in a holy place. ³² And Aaron and his sons shall eat the flesh of the ram and the bread that is in the basket in the entrance of the tent of meeting. ³³ They shall eat those things with which atonement was made at their ordination and consecration, but an outsider shall not eat of them, because they are holy. ³⁴ And if any of the flesh for the ordination or of the bread remain until the morning, then you shall burn the remainder with fire. It shall not be eaten, because it is holy.
>
> ³⁵ "Thus you shall do to Aaron and to his sons, according to all that I have commanded you. Through seven days shall you ordain them, ³⁶ and every day you shall offer a bull as a sin offering for atonement. Also you shall purify the altar, when you make atonement for it, and shall anoint it to consecrate it. ³⁷ Seven days you shall make atonement for the altar and consecrate it, and the altar shall be most holy. Whatever touches the altar shall become holy.
>
> ³⁸ "Now this is what you shall offer on the altar: two lambs a year old day by day regularly. ³⁹ One lamb you shall offer in the morning, and the other lamb you shall offer at twilight. ⁴⁰ And with the first lamb a tenth measure of fine flour mingled with a fourth of a hin of beaten oil, and a fourth of a hin of wine for a drink offering. ⁴¹ The other lamb you shall offer at twilight, and shall offer with it a grain offering and its drink offering, as in the morning, for a pleasing aroma, a food offering to the Lord. ⁴² It shall be a regular burnt of-

	OBSERVE	INTERPRET
fering throughout your generations at the entrance of the tent of meeting before the Lord, where I will meet with you, to speak to you there. ⁴³ There I will meet with the people of Israel, and it shall be sanctified by my glory. ⁴⁴ I will consecrate the tent of meeting and the altar. Aaron also and his sons I will consecrate to serve me as priests. ⁴⁵ I will dwell among the people of Israel and will be their God. ⁴⁶ And they shall know that I am the Lord their God, who brought them out of the land of Egypt that I might dwell among them. I am the Lord their God.		

| KEY WORDS | DEFINITIONS | CROSS REFERENCES |
|---|---|---|//

MAIN POINT(S)

APPLY

PRAY

day *three*

EXODUS 30:1-16

READ

¹ "You shall make an altar on which to burn incense; you shall make it of acacia wood. ² A cubit shall be its length, and a cubit its breadth. It shall be square, and two cubits shall be its height. Its horns shall be of one piece with it. ³ You shall overlay it with pure gold, its top and around its sides and its horns. And you shall make a molding of gold around it. ⁴ And you shall make two golden rings for it. Under its molding on two opposite sides of it you shall make them, and they shall be holders for poles with which to carry it. ⁵ You shall make the poles of acacia wood and overlay them with gold. ⁶ And you shall put it in front of the veil that is above the ark of the testimony, in front of the mercy seat that is above the testimony, where I will meet with you. ⁷ And Aaron shall burn fragrant incense on it. Every morning when he dresses the lamps he shall burn it, ⁸ and when Aaron sets up the lamps at twilight, he shall burn it, a regular incense offering before the Lord throughout your generations. ⁹ You shall not offer unauthorized incense on it, or a burnt offering, or a grain offering, and you shall not pour a drink offering on it. ¹⁰ Aaron shall make atonement on its horns once a year. With the blood of the sin offering of atonement he shall make atonement for it once in the year throughout your generations. It is most holy to the Lord."

¹¹ The Lord said to Moses, ¹² "When you take the census of the people of Israel, then each shall give a ransom for his life to the Lord when you number them, that there be no plague among them when you number them. ¹³ Each one who is numbered in the census shall give this: half a shekel according to the shekel of the sanctuary (the shekel is twenty gerahs), half a shekel as an offering to the Lord. ¹⁴ Everyone who is numbered in the census, from twenty years old and upward, shall give the Lord's offering. ¹⁵ The rich shall not give more, and the poor shall not give less, than the half shekel, when you give the Lord's offering to make atonement for your lives. ¹⁶ You shall take the atonement money from the people of Israel and shall give it for the service of the tent of meeting, that it may bring the people of Israel to remembrance before the Lord, so as to make atonement for your lives."

	OBSERVE	INTERPRET

| KEY WORDS | DEFINITIONS | CROSS REFERENCES |
|---|---|---|//

MAIN POINT(S)	APPLY

PRAY

day *four*

EXODUS 30:17-38

> ## READ
>
> ¹⁷ The Lord said to Moses, ¹⁸ "You shall also make a basin of bronze, with its stand of bronze, for washing. You shall put it between the tent of meeting and the altar, and you shall put water in it, ¹⁹ with which Aaron and his sons shall wash their hands and their feet. ²⁰ When they go into the tent of meeting, or when they come near the altar to minister, to burn a food offering to the Lord, they shall wash with water, so that they may not die. ²¹ They shall wash their hands and their feet, so that they may not die. It shall be a statute forever to them, even to him and to his offspring throughout their generations."
>
> ²² The Lord said to Moses, ²³ "Take the finest spices: of liquid myrrh 500 shekels, and of sweet-smelling cinnamon half as much, that is, 250, and 250 of aromatic cane, ²⁴ and 500 of cassia, according to the shekel of the sanctuary, and a hin of olive oil. ²⁵ And you shall make of these a sacred anointing oil blended as by the perfumer; it shall be a holy anointing oil. ²⁶ With it you shall anoint the tent of meeting and the ark of the testimony, ²⁷ and the table and all its utensils, and the lampstand and its utensils, and the altar of incense, ²⁸ and the altar of burnt offering with all its utensils and the basin and its stand. ²⁹ You shall consecrate them, that they may be most holy. Whatever touches them will become holy. ³⁰ You shall anoint Aaron and his sons, and consecrate them, that they may serve me as priests. ³¹ And you shall say to the people of Israel, 'This shall be my holy anointing oil throughout your generations. ³² It shall not be poured on the body of an ordinary person, and you shall make no other like it in composition. It is holy, and it shall be holy to you. ³³ Whoever compounds any like it or whoever puts any of it on an outsider shall be cut off from his people.'"
>
> ³⁴ The Lord said to Moses, "Take sweet spices, stacte, and onycha, and galbanum, sweet spices with pure frankincense (of each shall there be an equal part), ³⁵ and make an incense blended as by the perfumer, seasoned with salt, pure and holy. ³⁶ You shall beat some of it very small, and put part of it before the testimony in the tent of meeting where I shall meet with you. It shall be most holy for you. ³⁷ And the incense that you shall make according to its composition, you shall not make for yourselves. It shall be for you holy to the Lord. ³⁸ Whoever makes any like it to use as perfume shall be cut off from his people."

	OBSERVE	INTERPRET

KEY WORDS	DEFINITIONS	CROSS REFERENCES

MAIN POINT(S)	APPLY

PRAY

day *five*

EXODUS 29 & 30 | REVIEW & DISCUSSION QUESTIONS

1 Summary:	2 Write out your favorite verse from the passage, perhaps in your own words:
3 Define *consecrate*. Who does and who receives the consecrating? (29:44)	4 What animals and items are needed for the consecration ceremony? List the ordination offerings and share briefly what is involved.
5 The ordination involves a feast. (29:30-34) Explain who is able to take part and why.	6 What is the purpose of the regular burnt offerings?

7 Explain the purpose of the altar of incense. See the cross reference in Revelation 8:3. How might this also prefigure Christ? (See Hebrews 7:25.)

8 Is giving of the census offering mandatory? Who is to give and what is to be given? Explain why. (30:11-16)

9 Whether rich or poor, everyone paid the same amount for the census offering. How might this prefigure Christ's atonement for us?

10 Define *holy*. Is holiness relevant to our worship today? Explain.

11 Define *holy*. Is holiness relevant to living and worship today? Explain.

12 Worship God for the things you learned about Him in this chapter.

take it to *heart*

USE THIS SPACE TO WRITE OUT OR JOURNAL A FAVORITE VERSE OR PASSAGE FROM THIS WEEK'S STUDY

> SEE, I HAVE CALLED BY NAME
> BEZALEL THE SON OF URI,
> SON OF HUR, OF THE TRIBE
> OF JUDAH, AND I HAVE FILLED
> HIM WITH THE SPIRIT OF GOD...
>
> EXODUS 31:2

chapter *five*

EXODUS 31 & 32

take *note*

NOTES ON EXODUS 31 & 32

take *note*

NOTES ON EXODUS 31 & 32

day *one*

EXODUS 31:1-11

READ

¹ The Lord said to Moses, ² "See, I have called by name Bezalel the son of Uri, son of Hur, of the tribe of Judah, ³ and I have filled him with the Spirit of God, with ability and intelligence, with knowledge and all craftsmanship, ⁴ to devise artistic designs, to work in gold, silver, and bronze, ⁵ in cutting stones for setting, and in carving wood, to work in every craft. ⁶ And behold, I have appointed with him Oholiab, the son of Ahisamach, of the tribe of Dan. And I have given to all able men ability, that they may make all that I have commanded you: ⁷ the tent of meeting, and the ark of the testimony, and the mercy seat that is on it, and all the furnishings of the tent, ⁸ the table and its utensils, and the pure lampstand with all its utensils, and the altar of incense, ⁹ and the altar of burnt offering with all its utensils, and the basin and its stand, ¹⁰ and the finely worked garments, the holy garments for Aaron the priest and the garments of his sons, for their service as priests, ¹¹ and the anointing oil and the fragrant incense for the Holy Place. According to all that I have commanded you, they shall do."

OBSERVE

INTERPRET

KEY WORDS	DEFINITIONS	CROSS REFERENCES

MAIN POINT(S)	APPLY

PRAY

day *two*

EXODUS 31:12-18

READ

¹² And the Lord said to Moses, ¹³ "You are to speak to the people of Israel and say, 'Above all you shall keep my Sabbaths, for this is a sign between me and you throughout your generations, that you may know that I, the Lord, sanctify you. ¹⁴ You shall keep the Sabbath, because it is holy for you. Everyone who profanes it shall be put to death. Whoever does any work on it, that soul shall be cut off from among his people. ¹⁵ Six days shall work be done, but the seventh day is a Sabbath of solemn rest, holy to the Lord. Whoever does any work on the Sabbath day shall be put to death. ¹⁶ Therefore the people of Israel shall keep the Sabbath, observing the Sabbath throughout their generations, as a covenant forever. ¹⁷ It is a sign forever between me and the people of Israel that in six days the Lord made heaven and earth, and on the seventh day he rested and was refreshed.'"

¹⁸ And he gave to Moses, when he had finished speaking with him on Mount Sinai, the two tablets of the testimony, tablets of stone, written with the finger of God.

OBSERVE

INTERPRET

KEY WORDS	DEFINITIONS	CROSS REFERENCES

MAIN POINT(S)	APPLY

PRAY

day *three*

EXODUS 32:1-14

READ

¹ When the people saw that Moses delayed to come down from the mountain, the people gathered themselves together to Aaron and said to him, "Up, make us gods who shall go before us. As for this Moses, the man who brought us up out of the land of Egypt, we do not know what has become of him." ² So Aaron said to them, "Take off the rings of gold that are in the ears of your wives, your sons, and your daughters, and bring them to me." ³ So all the people took off the rings of gold that were in their ears and brought them to Aaron. ⁴ And he received the gold from their hand and fashioned it with a graving tool and made a golden calf. And they said, "These are your gods, O Israel, who brought you up out of the land of Egypt!" ⁵ When Aaron saw this, he built an altar before it. And Aaron made a proclamation and said, "Tomorrow shall be a feast to the Lord." ⁶ And they rose up early the next day and offered burnt offerings and brought peace offerings. And the people sat down to eat and drink and rose up to play.

⁷ And the Lord said to Moses, "Go down, for your people, whom you brought up out of the land of Egypt, have corrupted themselves. ⁸ They have turned aside quickly out of the way that I commanded them. They have made for themselves a golden calf and have worshiped it and sacrificed to it and said, 'These are your gods, O Israel, who brought you up out of the land of Egypt!'" ⁹ And the Lord said to Moses, "I have seen this people, and behold, it is a stiff-necked people. ¹⁰ Now therefore let me alone, that my wrath may burn hot against them and I may consume them, in order that I may make a great nation of you."

¹¹ But Moses implored the Lord his God and said, "O Lord, why does your wrath burn hot against your people, whom you have brought out of the land of Egypt with great power and with a mighty hand? ¹² Why should the Egyptians say, 'With evil intent did he bring them out, to kill them in the mountains and to consume them from the face of the earth'? Turn from your burning anger and relent from this disaster against your people. ¹³ Remember Abraham, Isaac, and Israel, your servants, to whom you swore by your own self, and said to them, 'I will multiply your offspring as the stars of heaven, and all this land that I have promised I will give to your offspring, and they shall inherit it forever.'" ¹⁴ And the Lord relented from the disaster that he had spoken of bringing on his people.

	OBSERVE	INTERPRET

KEY WORDS	DEFINITIONS	CROSS REFERENCES

MAIN POINT(S)	APPLY

PRAY

day *four*

EXODUS 32:15-35

> ## READ
>
> ¹⁵ Then Moses turned and went down from the mountain with the two tablets of the testimony in his hand, tablets that were written on both sides; on the front and on the back they were written. ¹⁶ The tablets were the work of God, and the writing was the writing of God, engraved on the tablets. ¹⁷ When Joshua heard the noise of the people as they shouted, he said to Moses, "There is a noise of war in the camp." ¹⁸ But he said, "It is not the sound of shouting for victory, or the sound of the cry of defeat, but the sound of singing that I hear." ¹⁹ And as soon as he came near the camp and saw the calf and the dancing, Moses' anger burned hot, and he threw the tablets out of his hands and broke them at the foot of the mountain. ²⁰ He took the calf that they had made and burned it with fire and ground it to powder and scattered it on the water and made the people of Israel drink it.
>
> ²¹ And Moses said to Aaron, "What did this people do to you that you have brought such a great sin upon them?" ²² And Aaron said, "Let not the anger of my lord burn hot. You know the people, that they are set on evil. ²³ For they said to me, 'Make us gods who shall go before us. As for this Moses, the man who brought us up out of the land of Egypt, we do not know what has become of him.' ²⁴ So I said to them, 'Let any who have gold take it off.' So they gave it to me, and I threw it into the fire, and out came this calf."
>
> ²⁵ And when Moses saw that the people had broken loose (for Aaron had let them break loose, to the derision of their enemies), ²⁶ then Moses stood in the gate of the camp and said, "Who is on the Lord's side? Come to me." And all the sons of Levi gathered around him. ²⁷ And he said to them, "Thus says the Lord God of Israel, 'Put your sword on your side each of you, and go to and fro from gate to gate throughout the camp, and each of you kill his brother and his companion and his neighbor.'" ²⁸ And the sons of Levi did according to the word of Moses. And that day about three thousand men of the people fell. ²⁹ And Moses said, "Today you have been ordained for the service of the Lord, each one at the cost of his son and of his brother, so that he might bestow a blessing upon you this day."
>
> ³⁰ The next day Moses said to the people, "You have sinned a great sin. And now I will go up to the Lord; perhaps I can make atonement for your sin." ³¹ So Moses returned to the Lord

	OBSERVE	INTERPRET
and said, "Alas, this people has sinned a great sin. They have made for themselves gods of gold. ³² But now, if you will forgive their sin—but if not, please blot me out of your book that you have written." ³³ But the Lord said to Moses, "Whoever has sinned against me, I will blot out of my book. ³⁴ But now go, lead the people to the place about which I have spoken to you; behold, my angel shall go before you. Nevertheless, in the day when I visit, I will visit their sin upon them." ³⁵ Then the Lord sent a plague on the people, because they made the calf, the one that Aaron made.		

KEY WORDS	DEFINITIONS	CROSS REFERENCES

MAIN POINT(S)	APPLY

PRAY

day *five*

EXODUS 31 & 32 | REVIEW & DISCUSSION QUESTIONS

1 Summary:	2 Write out your favorite verse from the passage, perhaps in your own words:
3 Notice how the work of God is to be done. (31:1-3) Who does the filling? (31:3) Define *filled*.	4 Apply. Do you rely on God's Spirit or your own abilities?
5 How is the creation of the tabernacle similar to the Creation story? (See Genesis 1:2.)	6 What is the purpose of the Sabbath?

7 Who is the giver of the covenant law? While Moses receives the law, Israel is breaking the first commandment. Explain.	8 What do the people demand of Aaron and why? Why do you think Aaron follows their request? What do we learn about the propensity of human heart?
9 Describe and explain God's reaction.	10 God deals graciously with His people throughout Exodus, but here we must acknowledge that apart from grace, sin leads to death. Apply. Are there other gods in your life? Pray.
11 What is the role of Moses? (31:11-13)	12 Worship God for the things you learned about Him in this chapter.

take it to *heart*

USE THIS SPACE TO WRITE OUT OR JOURNAL A FAVORITE VERSE OR PASSAGE FROM THIS WEEK'S STUDY

> "I WILL BE GRACIOUS TO WHOM I WILL BE GRACIOUS, AND WILL SHOW MERCY ON WHOM I WILL SHOW MERCY."
>
> EXODUS 33:19

chapter *six*

EXODUS 33 & 34

take *note*

NOTES ON EXODUS 33 & 34

take *note*

NOTES ON EXODUS 33 & 34

day *one*

EXODUS 33:1-11

READ

¹ The Lord said to Moses, "Depart; go up from here, you and the people whom you have brought up out of the land of Egypt, to the land of which I swore to Abraham, Isaac, and Jacob, saying, 'To your offspring I will give it.' ² I will send an angel before you, and I will drive out the Canaanites, the Amorites, the Hittites, the Perizzites, the Hivites, and the Jebusites. ³ Go up to a land flowing with milk and honey; but I will not go up among you, lest I consume you on the way, for you are a stiff-necked people."

⁴ When the people heard this disastrous word, they mourned, and no one put on his ornaments. ⁵ For the Lord had said to Moses, "Say to the people of Israel, 'You are a stiff-necked people; if for a single moment I should go up among you, I would consume you. So now take off your ornaments, that I may know what to do with you.'" ⁶ Therefore the people of Israel stripped themselves of their ornaments, from Mount Horeb onward.

⁷ Now Moses used to take the tent and pitch it outside the camp, far off from the camp, and he called it the tent of meeting. And everyone who sought the Lord would go out to the tent of meeting, which was outside the camp. ⁸ Whenever Moses went out to the tent, all the people would rise up, and each would stand at his tent door, and watch Moses until he had gone into the tent. ⁹ When Moses entered the tent, the pillar of cloud would descend and stand at the entrance of the tent, and the Lord would speak with Moses. ¹⁰ And when all the people saw the pillar of cloud standing at the entrance of the tent, all the people would rise up and worship, each at his tent door. ¹¹ Thus the Lord used to speak to Moses face to face, as a man speaks to his friend. When Moses turned again into the camp, his assistant Joshua the son of Nun, a young man, would not depart from the tent.

OBSERVE	INTERPRET

| KEY WORDS | DEFINITIONS | CROSS REFERENCES |
|---|---|---|//

MAIN POINT(S)	APPLY

PRAY

day *two*

EXODUS 33:12-23

READ

[12] Moses said to the Lord, "See, you say to me, 'Bring up this people,' but you have not let me know whom you will send with me. Yet you have said, 'I know you by name, and you have also found favor in my sight.' [13] Now therefore, if I have found favor in your sight, please show me now your ways, that I may know you in order to find favor in your sight. Consider too that this nation is your people." [14] And he said, "My presence will go with you, and I will give you rest." [15] And he said to him, "If your presence will not go with me, do not bring us up from here. [16] For how shall it be known that I have found favor in your sight, I and your people? Is it not in your going with us, so that we are distinct, I and your people, from every other people on the face of the earth?"

[17] And the Lord said to Moses, "This very thing that you have spoken I will do, for you have found favor in my sight, and I know you by name." [18] Moses said, "Please show me your glory." [19] And he said, "I will make all my goodness pass before you and will proclaim before you my name 'The Lord.' And I will be gracious to whom I will be gracious, and will show mercy on whom I will show mercy. [20] But," he said, "you cannot see my face, for man shall not see me and live." [21] And the Lord said, "Behold, there is a place by me where you shall stand on the rock, [22] and while my glory passes by I will put you in a cleft of the rock, and I will cover you with my hand until I have passed by. [23] Then I will take away my hand, and you shall see my back, but my face shall not be seen."

	OBSERVE	INTERPRET

KEY WORDS	DEFINITIONS	CROSS REFERENCES

MAIN POINT(S)	APPLY

PRAY

day *three*

EXODUS 34:1-16

> ### READ
>
> ¹ The Lord said to Moses, "Cut for yourself two tablets of stone like the first, and I will write on the tablets the words that were on the first tablets, which you broke. ² Be ready by the morning, and come up in the morning to Mount Sinai, and present yourself there to me on the top of the mountain. ³ No one shall come up with you, and let no one be seen throughout all the mountain. Let no flocks or herds graze opposite that mountain." ⁴ So Moses cut two tablets of stone like the first. And he rose early in the morning and went up on Mount Sinai, as the Lord had commanded him, and took in his hand two tablets of stone. ⁵ The Lord descended in the cloud and stood with him there, and proclaimed the name of the Lord. ⁶ The Lord passed before him and proclaimed, "The Lord, the Lord, a God merciful and gracious, slow to anger, and abounding in steadfast love and faithfulness, ⁷ keeping steadfast love for thousands, forgiving iniquity and transgression and sin, but who will by no means clear the guilty, visiting the iniquity of the fathers on the children and the children's children, to the third and the fourth generation." ⁸ And Moses quickly bowed his head toward the earth and worshiped. ⁹ And he said, "If now I have found favor in your sight, O Lord, please let the Lord go in the midst of us, for it is a stiff-necked people, and pardon our iniquity and our sin, and take us for your inheritance."
>
> ¹⁰ And he said, "Behold, I am making a covenant. Before all your people I will do marvels, such as have not been created in all the earth or in any nation. And all the people among whom you are shall see the work of the Lord, for it is an awesome thing that I will do with you.
>
> ¹¹ "Observe what I command you this day. Behold, I will drive out before you the Amorites, the Canaanites, the Hittites, the Perizzites, the Hivites, and the Jebusites. ¹² Take care, lest you make a covenant with the inhabitants of the land to which you go, lest it become a snare in your midst. ¹³ You shall tear down their altars and break their pillars and cut down their Asherim ¹⁴ (for you shall worship no other god, for the Lord, whose name is Jealous, is a jealous God), ¹⁵ lest you make a covenant with the inhabitants of the land, and when they whore after their gods and sacrifice to their gods and you are invited, you eat of his sacrifice, ¹⁶ and you take of their daughters for your sons, and their daughters whore after their gods and make your sons whore after their gods.

OBSERVE	INTERPRET

KEY WORDS	DEFINITIONS	CROSS REFERENCES

MAIN POINT(S)	APPLY

PRAY

day *four*
EXODUS 34:17-35

READ

17 "You shall not make for yourself any gods of cast metal.

18 "You shall keep the Feast of Unleavened Bread. Seven days you shall eat unleavened bread, as I commanded you, at the time appointed in the month Abib, for in the month Abib you came out from Egypt. 19 All that open the womb are mine, all your male livestock, the firstborn of cow and sheep. 20 The firstborn of a donkey you shall redeem with a lamb, or if you will not redeem it you shall break its neck. All the firstborn of your sons you shall redeem. And none shall appear before me empty-handed.

21 "Six days you shall work, but on the seventh day you shall rest. In plowing time and in harvest you shall rest. 22 You shall observe the Feast of Weeks, the firstfruits of wheat harvest, and the Feast of Ingathering at the year's end. 23 Three times in the year shall all your males appear before the Lord God, the God of Israel. 24 For I will cast out nations before you and enlarge your borders; no one shall covet your land, when you go up to appear before the Lord your God three times in the year.

25 "You shall not offer the blood of my sacrifice with anything leavened, or let the sacrifice of the Feast of the Passover remain until the morning. 26 The best of the firstfruits of your ground you shall bring to the house of the Lord your God. You shall not boil a young goat in its mother's milk."

27 And the Lord said to Moses, "Write these words, for in accordance with these words I have made a covenant with you and with Israel." 28 So he was there with the Lord forty days and forty nights. He neither ate bread nor drank water. And he wrote on the tablets the words of the covenant, the Ten Commandments.

29 When Moses came down from Mount Sinai, with the two tablets of the testimony in his hand as he came down from the mountain, Moses did not know that the skin of his face shone because he had been talking with God. 30 Aaron and all the people of Israel saw Moses, and behold, the skin of his face shone, and they were afraid to come near him. 31

	OBSERVE	INTERPRET
But Moses called to them, and Aaron and all the leaders of the congregation returned to him, and Moses talked with them. ³² Afterward all the people of Israel came near, and he commanded them all that the Lord had spoken with him in Mount Sinai. ³³ And when Moses had finished speaking with them, he put a veil over his face. ³⁴ Whenever Moses went in before the Lord to speak with him, he would remove the veil, until he came out. And when he came out and told the people of Israel what he was commanded, ³⁵ the people of Israel would see the face of Moses, that the skin of Moses' face was shining. And Moses would put the veil over his face again, until he went in to speak with him.		

KEY WORDS	DEFINITIONS	CROSS REFERENCES

MAIN POINT(S)	APPLY

PRAY

day *five*

EXODUS 33 & 34 | REVIEW & DISCUSSION QUESTIONS

1 Summary:	2 Write out your favorite verse from the passage, perhaps in your own words:
3 After their great sin, list any changes you notice in the relationship between God and the people.	4 What is God's command? (See Genesis 33:1.) To whom has God promised this land?
5 Explain the purpose of the tent of meeting.	6 Describe the scene of Moses going to the tent of meeting. Where are the people and how do they respond?

7 What do you learn from Moses's prayer? (33:12-18)

8 Define *glory*. How do Moses and the people experience God's glory? Can we experience God's glory today? Explain.

9 What is Moses's main concern and request of God? (34:9) Is this your main prayer concern? Ponder.

10 What is God's main concern for His people? (34:12-16)

11 Explain the significance of Moses's face shining after meeting with the Lord.

12 Worship God for the things you learned about Him in this chapter.

take it to *heart*

USE THIS SPACE TO WRITE OUT OR JOURNAL A FAVORITE VERSE OR PASSAGE FROM THIS WEEK'S STUDY

"THESE ARE THE THINGS THAT THE LORD HAS COMMANDED YOU TO DO."

EXODUS 35:1

chapter *seven*

EXODUS 35 & 36

take *note*

NOTES ON EXODUS 35 & 36

take *note*

NOTES ON EXODUS 35 & 36

day *one*

EXODUS 35:1-19

READ

¹ Moses assembled all the congregation of the people of Israel and said to them, "These are the things that the Lord has commanded you to do. ² Six days work shall be done, but on the seventh day you shall have a Sabbath of solemn rest, holy to the Lord. Whoever does any work on it shall be put to death. ³ You shall kindle no fire in all your dwelling places on the Sabbath day."

⁴ Moses said to all the congregation of the people of Israel, "This is the thing that the Lord has commanded. ⁵ Take from among you a contribution to the Lord. Whoever is of a generous heart, let him bring the Lord's contribution: gold, silver, and bronze; ⁶ blue and purple and scarlet yarns and fine twined linen; goats' hair, ⁷ tanned rams' skins, and goatskins; acacia wood, ⁸ oil for the light, spices for the anointing oil and for the fragrant incense, ⁹ and onyx stones and stones for setting, for the ephod and for the breastpiece.

¹⁰ "Let every skillful craftsman among you come and make all that the Lord has commanded: ¹¹ the tabernacle, its tent and its covering, its hooks and its frames, its bars, its pillars, and its bases; ¹² the ark with its poles, the mercy seat, and the veil of the screen; ¹³ the table with its poles and all its utensils, and the bread of the Presence; ¹⁴ the lampstand also for the light, with its utensils and its lamps, and the oil for the light; ¹⁵ and the altar of incense, with its poles, and the anointing oil and the fragrant incense, and the screen for the door, at the door of the tabernacle; ¹⁶ the altar of burnt offering, with its grating of bronze, its poles, and all its utensils, the basin and its stand; ¹⁷ the hangings of the court, its pillars and its bases, and the screen for the gate of the court; ¹⁸ the pegs of the tabernacle and the pegs of the court, and their cords; ¹⁹ the finely worked garments for ministering in the Holy Place, the holy garments for Aaron the priest, and the garments of his sons, for their service as priests."

OBSERVE	INTERPRET

| KEY WORDS | DEFINITIONS | CROSS REFERENCES |

| MAIN POINT(S) | APPLY |

PRAY

day *two*

EXODUS 35:20-35

> ### READ
>
> ²⁰ Then all the congregation of the people of Israel departed from the presence of Moses. ²¹ And they came, everyone whose heart stirred him, and everyone whose spirit moved him, and brought the Lord's contribution to be used for the tent of meeting, and for all its service, and for the holy garments. ²² So they came, both men and women. All who were of a willing heart brought brooches and earrings and signet rings and armlets, all sorts of gold objects, every man dedicating an offering of gold to the Lord. ²³ And every one who possessed blue or purple or scarlet yarns or fine linen or goats' hair or tanned rams' skins or goatskins brought them. ²⁴ Everyone who could make a contribution of silver or bronze brought it as the Lord's contribution. And every one who possessed acacia wood of any use in the work brought it. ²⁵ And every skillful woman spun with her hands, and they all brought what they had spun in blue and purple and scarlet yarns and fine twined linen. ²⁶ All the women whose hearts stirred them to use their skill spun the goats' hair. ²⁷ And the leaders brought onyx stones and stones to be set, for the ephod and for the breastpiece, ²⁸ and spices and oil for the light, and for the anointing oil, and for the fragrant incense. ²⁹ All the men and women, the people of Israel, whose heart moved them to bring anything for the work that the Lord had commanded by Moses to be done brought it as a freewill offering to the Lord.
>
> ³⁰ Then Moses said to the people of Israel, "See, the Lord has called by name Bezalel the son of Uri, son of Hur, of the tribe of Judah; ³¹ and he has filled him with the Spirit of God, with skill, with intelligence, with knowledge, and with all craftsmanship, ³² to devise artistic designs, to work in gold and silver and bronze, ³³ in cutting stones for setting, and in carving wood, for work in every skilled craft. ³⁴ And he has inspired him to teach, both him and Oholiab the son of Ahisamach of the tribe of Dan. ³⁵ He has filled them with skill to do every sort of work done by an engraver or by a designer or by an embroiderer in blue and purple and scarlet yarns and fine twined linen, or by a weaver—by any sort of workman or skilled designer.

	OBSERVE	INTERPRET

KEY WORDS	DEFINITIONS	CROSS REFERENCES

MAIN POINT(S)	APPLY

PRAY

day *three*

EXODUS 36:1-19

> ### READ
>
> [1] "Bezalel and Oholiab and every craftsman in whom the Lord has put skill and intelligence to know how to do any work in the construction of the sanctuary shall work in accordance with all that the Lord has commanded."
>
> [2] And Moses called Bezalel and Oholiab and every craftsman in whose mind the Lord had put skill, everyone whose heart stirred him up to come to do the work. [3] And they received from Moses all the contribution that the people of Israel had brought for doing the work on the sanctuary. They still kept bringing him freewill offerings every morning, [4] so that all the craftsmen who were doing every sort of task on the sanctuary came, each from the task that he was doing, [5] and said to Moses, "The people bring much more than enough for doing the work that the Lord has commanded us to do." [6] So Moses gave command, and word was proclaimed throughout the camp, "Let no man or woman do anything more for the contribution for the sanctuary." So the people were restrained from bringing, [7] for the material they had was sufficient to do all the work, and more.
>
> [8] And all the craftsmen among the workmen made the tabernacle with ten curtains. They were made of fine twined linen and blue and purple and scarlet yarns, with cherubim skillfully worked. [9] The length of each curtain was twenty-eight cubits, and the breadth of each curtain four cubits. All the curtains were the same size.
>
> [10] He coupled five curtains to one another, and the other five curtains he coupled to one another. [11] He made loops of blue on the edge of the outermost curtain of the first set. Likewise he made them on the edge of the outermost curtain of the second set. [12] He made fifty loops on the one curtain, and he made fifty loops on the edge of the curtain that was in the second set. The loops were opposite one another. [13] And he made fifty clasps of gold, and coupled the curtains one to the other with clasps. So the tabernacle was a single whole.
>
> [14] He also made curtains of goats' hair for a tent over the tabernacle. He made eleven curtains. [15] The length of each curtain was thirty cubits, and the breadth of each curtain four cubits. The eleven curtains were the same size. [16] He coupled five curtains by themselves,

and six curtains by them-selves. ¹⁷ And he made fifty loops on the edge of the outermost curtain of the one set, and fifty loops on the edge of the other connecting curtain. ¹⁸ And he made fifty clasps of bronze to couple the tent together that it might be a single whole.
¹⁹ And he made for the tent a covering of tanned rams' skins and goatskins.

OBSERVE	INTERPRET

KEY WORDS	DEFINITIONS	CROSS REFERENCES

MAIN POINT(S)	APPLY

PRAY

day *four*

EXODUS 36:20-38

READ

20 Then he made the upright frames for the tabernacle of acacia wood. 21 Ten cubits was the length of a frame, and a cubit and a half the breadth of each frame. 22 Each frame had two tenons for fitting together. He did this for all the frames of the tabernacle. 23 The frames for the tabernacle he made thus: twenty frames for the south side. 24 And he made forty bases of silver under the twenty frames, two bases under one frame for its two tenons, and two bases under the next frame for its two tenons. 25 For the second side of the tabernacle, on the north side, he made twenty frames 26 and their forty bases of silver, two bases under one frame and two bases under the next frame. 27 For the rear of the tabernacle westward he made six frames. 28 He made two frames for corners of the tabernacle in the rear. 29 And they were separate beneath but joined at the top, at the first ring. He made two of them this way for the two corners. 30 There were eight frames with their bases of silver: sixteen bases, under every frame two bases.

31 He made bars of acacia wood, five for the frames of the one side of the tabernacle, 32 and five bars for the frames of the other side of the tabernacle, and five bars for the frames of the tabernacle at the rear westward. 33 And he made the middle bar to run from end to end halfway up the frames. 34 And he overlaid the frames with gold, and made their rings of gold for holders for the bars, and overlaid the bars with gold.

35 He made the veil of blue and purple and scarlet yarns and fine twined linen; with cherubim skillfully worked into it he made it. 36 And for it he made four pillars of acacia and overlaid them with gold. Their hooks were of gold, and he cast for them four bases of silver. 37 He also made a screen for the entrance of the tent, of blue and purple and scarlet yarns and fine twined linen, embroidered with needlework, 38 and its five pillars with their hooks. He overlaid their capitals, and their fillets were of gold, but their five bases were of bronze.

	OBSERVE	INTERPRET

KEY WORDS	DEFINITIONS	CROSS REFERENCES

MAIN POINT(S)	APPLY

PRAY

day *five*

EXODUS 35 & 36 | REVIEW & DISCUSSION QUESTIONS

1 Summary:	2 Write out your favorite verse from the passage, perhaps in your own words:
3 Explain the purpose of the Sabbath. How do the Sabbath and worship go together? (35:1-3)	4 Define *generous heart* and explain how many have generous hearts. (Read Exodus 35:4-9 and Exodus 35:20-29.)
5 Having been slaves in Egypt, how do the Israelites have valuables to give? Why would it be difficult to give away their treasures?	6 Explain how generous hearts and worship go together. Apply.

7 In what way does God prepare Bezalel to head the building of the tabernacle? By whose power will the work be done?

8 In what way(s) has God gifted you with skill and intelligence to do the work that you do? Thank Him.

9 How is the work of Bezalel and the skilled workers to be done? (36:1) Share the importance of obedience in relation to worship.

10 Describe the enthusiasm of the people for this sanctuary project. Apply.

11 *He made* is repeated over and over again. Explain the significance.

12 Worship God for the things you learned about Him in this chapter.

take it to *heart*

USE THIS SPACE TO WRITE OUT OR JOURNAL A FAVORITE VERSE OR PASSAGE FROM THIS WEEK'S STUDY

BEHOLD, I SEND AN ANGEL BEFORE YOU TO GUARD YOU ON THE WAY AND TO BRING YOU TO THE PLACE THAT I HAVE PREPARED.

EXODUS 23:20

chapter *eight*

EXODUS 37 & 38

take *note*

NOTES ON EXODUS 37 & 38

take *note*

NOTES ON EXODUS 37 & 38

day *one*

EXODUS 37:1-16

READ

¹ Bezalel made the ark of acacia wood. Two cubits and a half was its length, a cubit and a half its breadth, and a cubit and a half its height. ² And he overlaid it with pure gold inside and outside, and made a molding of gold around it. ³ And he cast for it four rings of gold for its four feet, two rings on its one side and two rings on its other side. ⁴ And he made poles of acacia wood and overlaid them with gold ⁵ and put the poles into the rings on the sides of the ark to carry the ark. ⁶ And he made a mercy seat of pure gold. Two cubits and a half was its length, and a cubit and a half its breadth. ⁷ And he made two cherubim of gold. He made them of hammered work on the two ends of the mercy seat, ⁸ one cherub on the one end, and one cherub on the other end. Of one piece with the mercy seat he made the cherubim on its two ends. ⁹ The cherubim spread out their wings above, overshadowing the mercy seat with their wings, with their faces one to another; toward the mercy seat were the faces of the cherubim.

¹⁰ He also made the table of acacia wood. Two cubits was its length, a cubit its breadth, and a cubit and a half its height. ¹¹ And he overlaid it with pure gold, and made a molding of gold around it. ¹² And he made a rim around it a handbreadth wide, and made a molding of gold around the rim. ¹³ He cast for it four rings of gold and fastened the rings to the four corners at its four legs. ¹⁴ Close to the frame were the rings, as holders for the poles to carry the table. ¹⁵ He made the poles of acacia wood to carry the table, and overlaid them with gold. ¹⁶ And he made the vessels of pure gold that were to be on the table, its plates and dishes for incense, and its bowls and flagons with which to pour drink offerings.

| OBSERVE | INTERPRET |

| KEY WORDS | DEFINITIONS | CROSS REFERENCES |

| MAIN POINT(S) | APPLY |

PRAY

day *two*

EXODUS 37:17-29

READ

¹⁷ He also made the lampstand of pure gold. He made the lampstand of hammered work. Its base, its stem, its cups, its calyxes, and its flowers were of one piece with it. ¹⁸ And there were six branches going out of its sides, three branches of the lampstand out of one side of it and three branches of the lampstand out of the other side of it; ¹⁹ three cups made like almond blossoms, each with calyx and flower, on one branch, and three cups made like almond blossoms, each with calyx and flower, on the other branch—so for the six branches going out of the lampstand. ²⁰ And on the lampstand itself were four cups made like almond blossoms, with their calyxes and flowers, ²¹ and a calyx of one piece with it under each pair of the six branches going out of it. ²² Their calyxes and their branches were of one piece with it. The whole of it was a single piece of hammered work of pure gold. ²³ And he made its seven lamps and its tongs and its trays of pure gold. ²⁴ He made it and all its utensils out of a talent of pure gold.

²⁵ He made the altar of incense of acacia wood. Its length was a cubit, and its breadth was a cubit. It was square, and two cubits was its height. Its horns were of one piece with it. ²⁶ He overlaid it with pure gold, its top and around its sides and its horns. And he made a molding of gold around it, ²⁷ and made two rings of gold on it under its molding, on two opposite sides of it, as holders for the poles with which to carry it. ²⁸ And he made the poles of acacia wood and overlaid them with gold.

²⁹ He made the holy anointing oil also, and the pure fragrant incense, blended as by the perfumer.

	OBSERVE	INTERPRET

KEY WORDS	DEFINITIONS	CROSS REFERENCES

MAIN POINT(S)	APPLY

PRAY

day *three*

EXODUS 38:1-20

READ

¹ He made the altar of burnt offering of acacia wood. Five cubits was its length, and five cubits its breadth. It was square, and three cubits was its height. ² He made horns for it on its four corners. Its horns were of one piece with it, and he overlaid it with bronze. ³ And he made all the utensils of the altar, the pots, the shovels, the basins, the forks, and the fire pans. He made all its utensils of bronze. ⁴ And he made for the altar a grating, a network of bronze, under its ledge, extending halfway down. ⁵ He cast four rings on the four corners of the bronze grating as holders for the poles. ⁶ He made the poles of acacia wood and overlaid them with bronze. ⁷ And he put the poles through the rings on the sides of the altar to carry it with them. He made it hollow, with boards.

⁸ He made the basin of bronze and its stand of bronze, from the mirrors of the ministering women who ministered in the entrance of the tent of meeting.

⁹ And he made the court. For the south side the hangings of the court were of fine twined linen, a hundred cubits; ¹⁰ their twenty pillars and their twenty bases were of bronze, but the hooks of the pillars and their fillets were of silver. ¹¹ And for the north side there were hangings of a hundred cubits; their twenty pillars and their twenty bases were of bronze, but the hooks of the pillars and their fillets were of silver. ¹² And for the west side were hangings of fifty cubits, their ten pillars, and their ten bases; the hooks of the pillars and their fillets were of silver. ¹³ And for the front to the east, fifty cubits. ¹⁴ The hangings for one side of the gate were fifteen cubits, with their three pillars and three bases. ¹⁵ And so for the other side. On both sides of the gate of the court were hangings of fifteen cubits, with their three pillars and their three bases. ¹⁶ All the hangings around the court were of fine twined linen. ¹⁷ And the bases for the pillars were of bronze, but the hooks of the pillars and their fillets were of silver. The overlaying of their capitals was also of silver, and all the pillars of the court were filleted with silver. ¹⁸ And the screen for the gate of the court was embroidered with needlework in blue and purple and scarlet yarns and fine twined linen. It was twenty cubits long and five cubits high in its breadth, corresponding to the hangings of the court. ¹⁹ And their pillars were four in number. Their four bases were of

	OBSERVE	INTERPRET
bronze, their hooks of silver, and the overlaying of their capitals and their fillets of silver. ²⁰ And all the pegs for the tabernacle and for the court all around were of bronze.		

KEY WORDS	DEFINITIONS	CROSS REFERENCES

MAIN POINT(S)	APPLY

PRAY

day *four*
EXODUS 38:21-31

READ

²¹ These are the records of the tabernacle, the tabernacle of the testimony, as they were recorded at the commandment of Moses, the responsibility of the Levites under the direction of Ithamar the son of Aaron the priest. ²² Bezalel the son of Uri, son of Hur, of the tribe of Judah, made all that the Lord commanded Moses; ²³ and with him was Oholiab the son of Ahisamach, of the tribe of Dan, an engraver and designer and embroiderer in blue and purple and scarlet yarns and fine twined linen.

²⁴ All the gold that was used for the work, in all the construction of the sanctuary, the gold from the offering, was twenty-nine talents and 730 shekels, by the shekel of the sanctuary. ²⁵ The silver from those of the congregation who were recorded was a hundred talents and 1,775 shekels, by the shekel of the sanctuary: ²⁶ a beka a head (that is, half a shekel, by the shekel of the sanctuary), for everyone who was listed in the records, from twenty years old and upward, for 603,550 men. ²⁷ The hundred talents of silver were for casting the bases of the sanctuary and the bases of the veil; a hundred bases for the hundred talents, a talent a base. ²⁸ And of the 1,775 shekels he made hooks for the pillars and overlaid their capitals and made fillets for them. ²⁹ The bronze that was offered was seventy talents and 2,400 shekels; ³⁰ with it he made the bases for the entrance of the tent of meeting, the bronze altar and the bronze grating for it and all the utensils of the altar, ³¹ the bases around the court, and the bases of the gate of the court, all the pegs of the tabernacle, and all the pegs around the court.

	OBSERVE	INTERPRET

KEY WORDS	DEFINITIONS	CROSS REFERENCES

MAIN POINT(S)	APPLY

PRAY

day *five*

EXODUS 37 & 38 | REVIEW & DISCUSSION QUESTIONS

1 Summary:	2 Write out your favorite verse from the passage, perhaps in your own words:
3 Consider what Bezalel creates as he forms the ark and mercy seat. Explain the awesome significance of his work.	4 What do you learn about both God and Bezalel? (37:1-9)
5 What do you learn about Bezalel from the way he forms the table? (37:10-16)	6 What do you learn about Bezalel from his making of the lampstand and the altar of incense? (37:17-29) *Note: It's okay for your answer to be the same as before.*

7 Scripture specifically highlights who offers the bronze so that Bezalel can make the bronze basin. Explain.

8 What can we discern of their hearts? Apply. (38:8)

9 According to Exodus 38:21-26, who all has a part in making the tabernacle? Describe their roles.

10 Again, remembering that the Israelites are redeemed slaves, consider the expense of making the tabernacle. How might we be inspired by them in our worship today?

11 As you read the description of the materials, design, and skill used for making the tabernacle, what do you learn of God's heart?

12 Worship God for the things you learned about Him in this chapter.

take it to *heart*

USE THIS SPACE TO WRITE OUT OR JOURNAL A FAVORITE VERSE OR PASSAGE FROM THIS WEEK'S STUDY

HE MADE THE BASIN OF BRONZE AND ITS STAND OF BRONZE, FROM THE MIRRORS OF THE MINISTERING WOMEN WHO MINISTERED IN THE ENTRANCE OF THE TENT OF MEETING.

EXODUS 38:8

chapter *nine*

EXODUS 39 & 40

take *note*

NOTES ON EXODUS 39 & 40

take *note*

NOTES ON EXODUS 39 & 40

day *one*

EXODUS 39:1-21

> ## READ
>
> ¹ From the blue and purple and scarlet yarns they made finely woven garments, for ministering in the Holy Place. They made the holy garments for Aaron, as the Lord had commanded Moses.
>
> ² He made the ephod of gold, blue and purple and scarlet yarns, and fine twined linen. ³ And they hammered out gold leaf, and he cut it into threads to work into the blue and purple and the scarlet yarns, and into the fine twined linen, in skilled design. ⁴ They made for the ephod attaching shoulder pieces, joined to it at its two edges. ⁵ And the skillfully woven band on it was of one piece with it and made like it, of gold, blue and purple and scarlet yarns, and fine twined linen, as the Lord had commanded Moses.
>
> ⁶ They made the onyx stones, enclosed in settings of gold filigree, and engraved like the engravings of a signet, according to the names of the sons of Israel. ⁷ And he set them on the shoulder pieces of the ephod to be stones of remembrance for the sons of Israel, as the Lord had commanded Moses.
>
> ⁸ He made the breastpiece, in skilled work, in the style of the ephod, of gold, blue and purple and scarlet yarns, and fine twined linen. ⁹ It was square. They made the breastpiece doubled, a span its length and a span its breadth when doubled. ¹⁰ And they set in it four rows of stones. A row of sardius, topaz, and carbuncle was the first row; ¹¹ and the second row, an emerald, a sapphire, and a diamond; ¹² and the third row, a jacinth, an agate, and an amethyst; ¹³ and the fourth row, a beryl, an onyx, and a jasper. They were enclosed in settings of gold filigree. ¹⁴ There were twelve stones with their names according to the names of the sons of Israel. They were like signets, each engraved with its name, for the twelve tribes. ¹⁵ And they made on the breastpiece twisted chains like cords, of pure gold. ¹⁶ And they made two settings of gold filigree and two gold rings, and put the two rings on the two edges of the breastpiece. ¹⁷ And they put the two cords of gold in the two rings at the edges of the breastpiece. ¹⁸ They attached the two ends of the two cords to the two settings of filigree. Thus they attached it in front to the shoulder pieces of the ephod. ¹⁹ Then they made two rings of gold, and put them at the two ends of the breastpiece, on its inside edge next to

	OBSERVE	INTERPRET
the ephod. ²⁰ And they made two rings of gold, and attached them in front to the lower part of the two shoulder pieces of the ephod, at its seam above the skillfully woven band of the ephod. ²¹ And they bound the breastpiece by its rings to the rings of the ephod with a lace of blue, so that it should lie on the skillfully woven band of the ephod, and that the breastpiece should not come loose from the ephod, as the Lord had commanded Moses.		

KEY WORDS	DEFINITIONS	CROSS REFERENCES

MAIN POINT(S)	APPLY

PRAY

day *two*

EXODUS 39:22-43

> ### READ
>
> ²² He also made the robe of the ephod woven all of blue, ²³ and the opening of the robe in it was like the opening in a garment, with a binding around the opening, so that it might not tear. ²⁴ On the hem of the robe they made pomegranates of blue and purple and scarlet yarns and fine twined linen. ²⁵ They also made bells of pure gold, and put the bells between the pomegranates all around the hem of the robe, between the pomegranates— ²⁶ a bell and a pomegranate, a bell and a pomegranate around the hem of the robe for ministering, as the Lord had commanded Moses.
>
> ²⁷ They also made the coats, woven of fine linen, for Aaron and his sons, ²⁸ and the turban of fine linen, and the caps of fine linen, and the linen undergarments of fine twined linen, ²⁹ and the sash of fine twined linen and of blue and purple and scarlet yarns, embroidered with needlework, as the Lord had commanded Moses.
>
> ³⁰ They made the plate of the holy crown of pure gold, and wrote on it an inscription, like the engraving of a signet, "Holy to the Lord." ³¹ And they tied to it a cord of blue to fasten it on the turban above, as the Lord had commanded Moses.
>
> ³² Thus all the work of the tabernacle of the tent of meeting was finished, and the people of Israel did according to all that the Lord had commanded Moses; so they did. ³³ Then they brought the tabernacle to Moses, the tent and all its utensils, its hooks, its frames, its bars, its pillars, and its bases; ³⁴ the covering of tanned rams' skins and goatskins, and the veil of the screen; ³⁵ the ark of the testimony with its poles and the mercy seat; ³⁶ the table with all its utensils, and the bread of the Presence; ³⁷ the lampstand of pure gold and its lamps with the lamps set and all its utensils, and the oil for the light; ³⁸ the golden altar, the anointing oil and the fragrant incense, and the screen for the entrance of the tent; ³⁹ the bronze altar, and its grating of bronze, its poles, and all its utensils; the basin and its stand; ⁴⁰ the hangings of the court, its pillars, and its bases, and the screen for the gate of the court, its cords, and its pegs; and all the utensils for the service of the tabernacle, for the tent of meeting; ⁴¹ the finely worked garments for ministering in the Holy Place, the holy garments for Aaron the priest, and the garments of his sons for their

	OBSERVE	INTERPRET
service as priests. ⁴² According to all that the Lord had commanded Moses, so the people of Israel had done all the work. ⁴³ And Moses saw all the work, and behold, they had done it; as the Lord had commanded, so had they done it. Then Moses blessed them.		

KEY WORDS	DEFINITIONS	CROSS REFERENCES

MAIN POINT(S)	APPLY

PRAY

day *three*

EXODUS 40:1-15

> ### READ
>
> [1] The Lord spoke to Moses, saying, [2] "On the first day of the first month you shall erect the tabernacle of the tent of meeting. [3] And you shall put in it the ark of the testimony, and you shall screen the ark with the veil. [4] And you shall bring in the table and arrange it, and you shall bring in the lampstand and set up its lamps. [5] And you shall put the golden altar for incense before the ark of the testimony, and set up the screen for the door of the tabernacle. [6] You shall set the altar of burnt offering before the door of the tabernacle of the tent of meeting, [7] and place the basin between the tent of meeting and the altar, and put water in it. [8] And you shall set up the court all around, and hang up the screen for the gate of the court.
>
> [9] "Then you shall take the anointing oil and anoint the tabernacle and all that is in it, and consecrate it and all its furniture, so that it may become holy. [10] You shall also anoint the altar of burnt offering and all its utensils, and consecrate the altar, so that the altar may become most holy. [11] You shall also anoint the basin and its stand, and consecrate it. [12] Then you shall bring Aaron and his sons to the entrance of the tent of meeting and shall wash them with water [13] and put on Aaron the holy garments. And you shall anoint him and consecrate him, that he may serve me as priest. [14] You shall bring his sons also and put coats on them, [15] and anoint them, as you anointed their father, that they may serve me as priests. And their anointing shall admit them to a perpetual priesthood throughout their generations."

	OBSERVE	INTERPRET

KEY WORDS	DEFINITIONS	CROSS REFERENCES

MAIN POINT(S)	APPLY

PRAY

day *four*

EXODUS 40:16-38

READ

¹⁶ This Moses did; according to all that the Lord commanded him, so he did. ¹⁷ In the first month in the second year, on the first day of the month, the tabernacle was erected. ¹⁸ Moses erected the tabernacle. He laid its bases, and set up its frames, and put in its poles, and raised up its pillars. ¹⁹ And he spread the tent over the tabernacle and put the covering of the tent over it, as the Lord had commanded Moses. ²⁰ He took the testimony and put it into the ark, and put the poles on the ark and set the mercy seat above on the ark. ²¹ And he brought the ark into the tabernacle and set up the veil of the screen, and screened the ark of the testimony, as the Lord had commanded Moses. ²² He put the table in the tent of meeting, on the north side of the tabernacle, outside the veil, ²³ and arranged the bread on it before the Lord, as the Lord had commanded Moses. ²⁴ He put the lampstand in the tent of meeting, opposite the table on the south side of the tabernacle, ²⁵ and set up the lamps before the Lord, as the Lord had commanded Moses. ²⁶ He put the golden altar in the tent of meeting before the veil, ²⁷ and burned fragrant incense on it, as the Lord had commanded Moses. ²⁸ He put in place the screen for the door of the tabernacle. ²⁹ And he set the altar of burnt offering at the entrance of the tabernacle of the tent of meeting, and offered on it the burnt offering and the grain offering, as the Lord had commanded Moses. ³⁰ He set the basin between the tent of meeting and the altar, and put water in it for washing, ³¹ with which Moses and Aaron and his sons washed their hands and their feet. ³² When they went into the tent of meeting, and when they approached the altar, they washed, as the Lord commanded Moses. ³³ And he erected the court around the tabernacle and the altar, and set up the screen of the gate of the court. So Moses finished the work.

³⁴ Then the cloud covered the tent of meeting, and the glory of the Lord filled the tabernacle. ³⁵ And Moses was not able to enter the tent of meeting because the cloud settled on it, and the glory of the Lord filled the tabernacle. ³⁶ Throughout all their journeys, whenever the cloud was taken up from over the tabernacle, the people of Israel would set out. ³⁷ But if the cloud was not taken up, then they did not set out till the day that it was taken up. ³⁸ For the cloud of the Lord was on the tabernacle by day, and fire was in it by night, in the sight of all the house of Israel throughout all their journeys.

	OBSERVE	INTERPRET

KEY WORDS	DEFINITIONS	CROSS REFERENCES

MAIN POINT(S)	APPLY

PRAY

day *five*

EXODUS 39 & 40 | REVIEW & DISCUSSION QUESTIONS

1 Summary:	2 Write out your favorite verse from the passage, perhaps in your own words:
3 Much attention is given to the detail of making the priestly clothing. This is not intended to bore us, but to tell us something about God's heart. What do you learn?	4 What do we learn about those who made the garments and the hearts of the Israelites? (See Exodus 39:1 and 39:32.) Apply.
5 Describe Aaron's crown. What does it mean to be "holy to the Lord?" Does this statement represent Aaron himself or all of the Israelites?	6 Explain how all this relates to us today, the way we are to be clothed in Christ. Consider as you clothe yourself for the day.

7 Define *behold*. Explain what Moses wants everyone to see. (39:43) How important is obedience to God and worship?

8 What do the Israelites receive for doing all the work as the Lord had commanded? (39:42-43) Apply.

9 Define *anoint*. Everything and everyone used for the purpose of worshiping God is anointed. Is this applicable to us today? Explain.

10 What do you learn about Moses as he sets up the tabernacle? (See Exodus 40:33, Hebrews 3:2, and Hebrews 3:5.)

11 Explain the significance of the glory of the Lord filling the tabernacle. How would seeing this encourage and spur the Israelites to worship throughout all their journeys? Apply.

12 Worship God for the things you learned about Him in this chapter.

take it to *heart*

USE THIS SPACE TO WRITE OUT OR JOURNAL A FAVORITE VERSE OR PASSAGE FROM THIS WEEK'S STUDY

ACCORDING TO ALL THAT
THE LORD HAD COMMANDED
MOSES, SO THE PEOPLE OF
ISRAEL HAD DONE ALL THE WORK.

EXODUS 40:42

final *thoughts*

WRAPPING UP

final *thoughts*
WRAPPING UP | EXODUS 24-40

1 Choose your favorite verse from Exodus 24-40. Write it out here.	2 Why is this verse meaningful to you?
3 What overarching theme or themes did you notice throughout your study?	4 Provide a brief character analysis of Moses. Apply.
5 Provide a brief character analysis of the Israelites. Apply.	6 Explain how the Lord is the Hero of this story.

7 What have you personally learned about God through this study? Perhaps review the challenge verses of Exodus 34:6-7 and relate to this study.

8 Share what you learned about worship from this study.

9 How would you summarize Exodus 24-40 in one sentence? Could you summarize it in one word?

10 How does Exodus 24-40 fit into the "Big View" of the Bible and connect to the New Testament?

11 How has God transformed your heart through this study of Exodus 24-40? How will you live or think differently than before?

12 Praise God for at least one truth revealed in the course of this study.

final *thoughts*
WRAPPING UP | EXODUS 24-40

Congratulations! You did it!

Thank you for journeying with us in this **SIMPLY BIBLE** | EXODUS study. We hope and pray you are knowing and enjoying God in fresh ways.

We want to encourage you to keep going. In the beginning, we disclosed that this journey through Exodus is not a short one. In order to work our way through 40 chapters, this study is divided into three books. Each provides a window to a greater understanding of our God and His heart of mercy.

As a reminder, here is why each of the books is important:

> **Book 1 | Exodus 1-12**
> The LORD rescues. Call it redemption. Call it deliverance. We see God break the chains of His people and set them free.
>
> **Book 2 | Exodus 13-23**
> The LORD provides. Outside of Egypt, God has the back of His people. He miraculously brings life out of death at the Red Sea. He keeps them safe and provides for their needs in the wilderness.
>
> **Book 3 | Exodus 24-40**
> The LORD is present with His people. Footloose and fancy free, how should God's people live? How will God be worshipped? God graciously gives instructions.

This three-step format helps to paint a more thorough understanding of God's Word.

In order to keep it simple, each book of the **SIMPLY BIBLE** | EXODUS series is laid out in exactly the same way. This includes the same introduction and challenge. This repetition is purposeful and is intended to help us better know and enjoy the God of Exodus. The only variance within the books are the chapters of Scripture studied.

With excitement, we invite you to continue the journey with us!

AND THEY SHALL KNOW THAT
I AM THE LORD THEIR GOD, WHO
BROUGHT THEM OUT OF THE
LAND OF EGYPT THAT I MIGHT
DWELL AMONG THEM. I AM
THE LORD THEIR GOD.

EXODUS 29:46

leader *guide*

MAXIMIZING THE SMALL-GROUP EXPERIENCE

GO THEREFORE AND MAKE DISCIPLES OF ALL NATIONS, BAPTIZING THEM IN THE NAME OF THE FATHER AND OF THE SON AND OF THE HOLY SPIRIT, TEACHING THEM TO OBSERVE ALL THAT I HAVE COMMANDED YOU.

MATTHEW 28:19-20

introduction

LEADING WOMEN THROUGH **SIMPLY BIBLE**

Welcome to SIMPLY BIBLE! Thank you for your commitment to walk alongside a group of women for this season of drawing near to God through His Word. In the midst of uncertainty, anxiety, and the cares of this world, what better place to lead women than to Jesus, the Author and Perfector of our faith?

The primary objective of SIMPLY BIBLE is this:

> To inspire every woman to love God
> with all her heart, soul, mind and strength,
> and to love others as herself.
>
> LUKE 10:27

So breathe easy! Your role is simply to help facilitate that goal: to inspire women to love God and love others as herself. This does not entail becoming a walking commentary of Exodus. Rather, the qualifications involve loving God and His Word with a desire to love and care for His women. That's it. Did you catch that? The prerequisite for leading women through this study is not Bible knowledge, it's love. Success depends on the heart.

SO GUARD YOUR HEART.

Ethos is a Latin word that denotes the fundamental character or spirit of a community, group, or person. When used to discuss dramatic literature, ethos is that moral element used to determine a character's action rather than his or her thought or emotion.[1] Ethos points to the inward being, to the moral fabric of the heart. In Biblical language, ethos absolutely compares to a person's heart. And our ethos, our heart, is important to God.

His Word tells us:

> Above all else, guard your heart,
> for everything you do flows from it.
>
> PROVERBS 4:23 (NIV)

Above all else, guard your heart. Why? Because everything we do flows from the heart, from our inward being. And that "everything" includes leading women through God's Word. If we want to see women growing in authentic relationships with Christ and with one another, that process must first begin in our own hearts.

> For the Lord sees not as man sees: man looks on the
> outward appearance, but the Lord looks on the heart.
>
> 1 SAMUEL 16:7

As individuals, ministry groups, and even churches, we often focus on outward appearances. I'm guilty. I call it "dressing up and playing church." When more time is spent designing beautiful handouts, creating engaging social media posts, coordinating impeccable table decorations and other "outward" items versus time spent on heart preparation, it might signal a problem. There is nothing wrong with making the outward beautiful. Yet, God looks at the heart. Is our primary focus there, too?

---

[1] **ethos.** Dictionary.com. *Dictionary.com Unabridged.* Random House, Inc. http://www.dictionary.com/browse/ethos (accessed: March 16, 2018).

When women hurt, the externals mean very little. Aside from a comforting cup of tea or coffee, it's love and hope overflowing from the heart that make a difference. To overflow with love and hope, hearts must be tapped into the power of His Spirit and His Word.

To effectively "guard our hearts" and prepare to lead women in inductive Bible study, three things are necessary:

(1) Jesus
(2) Prayer
(3) The Word

GUARDING YOUR HEART WITH **JESUS**

This may seem obvious, even "in your face" obvious. But honestly, isn't it easy for us to miss the forest for the trees? How can we expect others to believe if we ourselves are not believing? How will others trust if we do not trust? Apart from Jesus, we will not overflow with His Spirit and hope. Our efforts will ring hollow. Paul puts it this way:

> If I speak in the tongues of men and of angels, but have not love, I am a noisy gong or a clanging cymbal.
>
> 1 CORINTHIANS 13:1

None of us wants to be an annoying gong gone wrong. But without a personal heart connection to Christ's heart of love, we labor in our own strength. One friend refers to this kind of fruit as the "fake grapes" found in her Grandma's kitchen. Instead, we're seeking the juicy-sweet fruit of the Spirit that comes from abiding in the True Vine:

> Abide in me, and I in you. As the branch cannot bear fruit by itself, unless it abides in the vine, neither can you, unless you abide in me.
>
> JOHN 15:4

Abiding in Jesus is the secret, powerful ingredient to leading Bible study. Okay, maybe it's not so secret, but it is powerful! Some days, we feel that heart connection with God and other days we do not. Abiding is not a feeling. We know we abide as we seek to obey and follow His will. Fruit will follow.

An effective leader unifies her heart with Christ's humble and authentic heart. Are you daily abiding and aligning your character to Jesus from the inside out? Godly transformation happens as a woman applies Scripture, yields to God's will, and allows for the Spirit's holy work to happen within her own heart. That leads to true beauty. It's super attractive. Others will desire this kind of beauty and follow. Peter says it this way:

> Let your adorning be the hidden person of the heart
> with the imperishable beauty of a gentle and quiet spirit,
> which in God's sight is very precious.
>
> 1 PETER 3:4

GUARDING YOUR HEART WITH **PRAYER**

Here again, the need for prayer is obvious. Yet sometimes when caught up in preparation details, we overlook the obvious. Pray, pray, and pray! If Jesus required prayer in order to remain united with His Father, we surely require it more. Prayer keeps us focused on Christ and helps us remember that He is the Good Shepherd who ultimately leads our flocks to green pastures and quiet waters. As we study His Word, He will guide us in paths of righteousness. However, without Christ paving the way and clearing the path, we will struggle to get there. And so, we pray.

Set aside individual time to pray for Bible study. Before the semester begins, consider setting aside one day to commune with God. Be. Listen. Share. Sing. Seek. Surrender. Ponder. Commit. Once Bible study begins, allow for time to pray together as a group. Recognizing that prayer might be new for some, remind women to simply share their hearts and relate with God. The acronym *P.R.A.Y.* provides an easy-to-follow template guiding groups through four steps of prayer:

P	PRAISE	Praise God for who He is.

> Blessed be the God and Father of our Lord Jesus Christ!
> *I Peter 1:3*

Short "popcorn prayers" of praise like Peter's easily allow everyone to participate. Simple words and phrases to worship God work best:

- I praise You, God, as the Light of the World.
- I praise You for You are Mighty to Save.
- Lord, You are Life.
- You are Truth.

Beginning group sessions with praise turns and focuses our hearts toward God.

R	REPENT	Confess and agree with God concerning sin.

> If we confess our sins, he is faithful and just to forgive us our sins and to cleanse us from all unrighteousness.
> *I John 1:9*

Offer group members a silent moment to allow for private confession.

A	ADORE	Admire and thank God for His ways.

> Give thanks in all circumstances; for this is the will of God in Christ Jesus for you.
> *I Thessalonians 5:18*

In the midst of trials, thanksgiving is a beautiful way to declare faith in God's goodness. Together, give thanks for all that God revealed during the study session.

Y	YIELD	Acknowledge your dependence on God. Yield to His ways.

> Humble yourselves, therefore, under the mighty hand of God so that at the proper time he may exalt you, casting all your anxieties on him, because he cares for you.
> *I Peter 5:6-7*

With Peter's encouragement, give every concern to the Lord!

With that, what sorts of things shall we yield to God? Here are a few ideas and ways to align with God's heart:

- May God be glorified through the study.
- May women begin to hunger and thirst for God and His Word.
- May God's will be accomplished in the hearts of women.
- May women believe in Jesus and cast their worries to Him.
- May women's hearts be united with His and with one another.
- May God offer protection from all distractions as women study His Word.
- May God's Word transform hearts and lives, that women would begin to think and live differently.

GUARDING YOUR HEART WITH **THE WORD**

Whether large group teaching or facilitating small group discussion, leaders are prone to fall into the trap of thinking that we need all the right answers. Furthermore, we think we need to be able to speak all those answers eloquently. Due to this false thinking, some leaders forget that love is the answer and spend countless hours scouring commentaries. They wear themselves out! God's Word is so deep and rich that the depths of a Scripture passage will not be plumbed in just one week. Thinking we need to have all the right answers is a fallacy.

Without a doubt, commentaries are valuable for checking one's interpretation. However, for leaders who spend too much time delving into commentaries versus pondering God's Word, the risk is that their workbooks and discussion will reflect the *commentaries* more than *Scripture itself*.

To counter this, we simply need time in God's Word. As we read, observe, and marinate in the Bible text itself, God's Spirit teaches and leads. His Word speaks on its own. It is powerful and effective. We can trust in it!

> So shall my word be that goes out from my mouth;
> it shall not return to me empty, but it shall
> accomplish that which I purpose, and shall
> succeed in the thing for which I sent it.
>
> ISAIAH 55:11

Read, read, and read again. As mentioned in the introduction, read the passage using various translations. Read aloud, and read slowly. Ponder. Listen to the Word while driving. Talk about what you are learning and discovering in the Word with family and friends. This will help you be prepared to speak when it is time for Bible study. Just as we marinate meat to soften, tenderize, and flavor it, we "sit in" the text, allowing God's Spirit to soften, tenderize, and flavor our hearts and minds with His personal message.

> I have stored up your word in my heart,
> that I might not sin against you.
>
> PSALM 119:11

A challenging, but brilliant way to soak in Scripture is memorization. Memorization is hard work, but the payoff is great. Scripture becomes embedded within our hearts and overflows when needed. Memorized scriptures guard my own heart. In leading, I have noticed that reciting or praying Scripture over women deeply touches their hearts, too. I highly encourage memorizing at least one key verse or passage from the study.

Ideally, teachers and small group leaders should prepare the study a week ahead of time. Yep! You read that right. Seek to be one week ahead of the regular study schedule in your personal study of the Word. If possible, allow time for leaders to review together before leading and teaching in groups the following week. The benefits of discussing, sharing, and grappling with the Word as leaders are priceless for preparation and confidence in facilitating discussion. Through it, God knits together the leaders' hearts. This will transform the *ethos* or heart of the group as a whole.

FRIENDS, MAY WE GUARD OUR HEARTS.

With Jesus, prayer and His Word, we are well-equipped to love and lead transformative conversations around our Bible study tables.

> But you will receive power when the Holy Spirit
> has come upon you, and you will be my witnesses
> in Jerusalem and in all Judea and Samaria,
> and to the end of the earth.
>
> ACTS 1:8

The following tools and resources included in this appendix may provide additional help and support as you endeavor to lead your group. Use them however you find them to be helpful.

- Effective Leadership Guide
- Weekly Preparation Guide
- Bible Study Schedule
- Small Group Roster
- Attendance Record
- Prayer Log

effective *leadership*

A GUIDE TO LEADING A SMALL GROUP EFFECTIVELY

Remember that the goal for our study is to see women growing in relationship with Christ and one another. You do not need to be a Bible expert to lead women in discussion about His Word. You only need a heart to love and encourage women. So, what does effective small group leadership look like?

ENCOURAGING | In an encouraging small group, all participants feel included and welcome to share freely. Thoughts and ideas are respected, and women are cheered on in their efforts to grow closer to God through their study of His Word.

BIBLICALLY SOUND | When we endeavor to create a biblically-sound environment, we point women in the direction of truth and correct doctrine, gently guiding them away from wrong thinking.

BALANCED | In a group that is balanced, shy or quiet women are drawn out and encouraged to participate in discussions, while "over-sharers" are encouraged to listen to others and not to dominate the conversation.

WISE | A wise small group leader recognizes when the conversation is getting off-topic or veering toward gossip. In such situations, it is a good idea to redirect women back to the ultimate focus of the meeting: God's Word.

PRAYERFUL | A prayerful group leader is an asset to her group. She prays regularly for her group members and facilitates opportunities for them to pray for one another.

CONFIDENTIAL | Group members should feel secure that the things they share will remain confidential. An effective small group leader is committed to preserving the privacy of her group members.

weekly preparation guide
PREPARING FOR SMALL-GROUP MEETINGS

WEEK 1: EXODUS 24

- ☐ Read the assigned daily passages.
- ☐ Use each daily framework to observe, interpret, and apply.
- ☐ Respond to all of the Day 5 questions.
- ☐ Pray for your small group meeting and for your group members.

1 What does this week's study tell me about God?	2 What does this week's study tell me about how I am to relate to Him?

WEEK 2: EXODUS 25 & 26

- ☐ Read the assigned daily passages.
- ☐ Use each daily framework to observe, interpret, and apply.
- ☐ Respond to all of the Day 5 questions.
- ☐ Pray for your small group meeting and for your group members.

1 What does this week's study tell me about God?	2 What does this week's study tell me about how I am to relate to Him?

WEEK 3: EXODUS 27 & 28

- [ ] Read the assigned daily passages.
- [ ] Use each daily framework to observe, interpret, and apply.
- [ ] Respond to all of the Day 5 questions.
- [ ] Pray for your small group meeting and for your group members.

1 What does this week's study tell me about God?	2 What does this week's study tell me about how I am to relate to Him?

WEEK 4: EXODUS 29 & 30

- [ ] Read the assigned daily passages.
- [ ] Use each daily framework to observe, interpret, and apply.
- [ ] Respond to all of the Day 5 questions.
- [ ] Pray for your small group meeting and for your group members.

1 What does this week's study tell me about God?	2 What does this week's study tell me about how I am to relate to Him?

WEEK 5: EXODUS 31 & 32

- [ ] Read the assigned daily passages.
- [ ] Use each daily framework to observe, interpret, and apply.
- [ ] Respond to all of the Day 5 questions.
- [ ] Pray for your small group meeting and for your group members.

1 What does this week's study tell me about God?	2 What does this week's study tell me about how I am to relate to Him?

WEEK 6: EXODUS 33 & 34

- [ ] Read the assigned daily passages.
- [ ] Use each daily framework to observe, interpret, and apply.
- [ ] Respond to all of the Day 5 questions.
- [ ] Pray for your small group meeting and for your group members.

1 What does this week's study tell me about God?	2 What does this week's study tell me about how I am to relate to Him?

WEEK 7: EXODUS 35 & 36

- ☐ Read the assigned daily passages.
- ☐ Use each daily framework to observe, interpret, and apply.
- ☐ Respond to all of the Day 5 questions.
- ☐ Pray for your small group meeting and for your group members.

1 What does this week's study tell me about God?	2 What does this week's study tell me about how I am to relate to Him?

WEEK 8: EXODUS 37 & 38

- ☐ Read the assigned daily passages.
- ☐ Use each daily framework to observe, interpret, and apply.
- ☐ Respond to all of the Day 5 questions.
- ☐ Pray for your small group meeting and for your group members.

1 What does this week's study tell me about God?	2 What does this week's study tell me about how I am to relate to Him?

WEEK 9: EXODUS 39 & 40

- ☐ Read the assigned daily passages.
- ☐ Use each daily framework to observe, interpret, and apply.
- ☐ Respond to all of the Day 5 questions.
- ☐ Pray for your small group meeting and for your group members.

1 What does this week's study tell me about God?	2 What does this week's study tell me about how I am to relate to Him?

WEEK 10: WRAPPING UP | FINAL THOUGHTS

- ☐ Read the assigned daily passages.
- ☐ Use each daily framework to observe, interpret, and apply.
- ☐ Respond to all of the Day 5 questions.
- ☐ Pray for your small group meeting and for your group members.

1 What does this week's study tell me about God?	2 What does this week's study tell me about how I am to relate to Him?

bible study *schedule*

EXODUS 24-40 | A **SIMPLY BIBLE** STUDY

	READING ASSIGNMENT	SMALL GROUP MEETING DATE	LEADER MEETING DATE
WEEK 1			
WEEK 2			
WEEK 3			
WEEK 4			
WEEK 5			
WEEK 6			
WEEK 7			
WEEK 8			
WEEK 9			
WEEK 10			

small group *roster*
EXODUS 24-40 | A **SIMPLY BIBLE** STUDY

PARTICIPANT LIST

1
2
3
4
5
6
7
8
9
10
11
12
13
14
15

NAME	
BIRTHDAY	
PHONE NUMBER	
EMAIL ADDRESS	
CONTACT METHOD	
NOTES	

NAME	
BIRTHDAY	
PHONE NUMBER	
EMAIL ADDRESS	
CONTACT METHOD	
NOTES	

NAME	
BIRTHDAY	
PHONE NUMBER	
EMAIL ADDRESS	
CONTACT METHOD	
NOTES	

NAME	
BIRTHDAY	
PHONE NUMBER	
EMAIL ADDRESS	
CONTACT METHOD	
NOTES	

NAME	
BIRTHDAY	
PHONE NUMBER	
EMAIL ADDRESS	
CONTACT METHOD	
NOTES	

NAME	
BIRTHDAY	
PHONE NUMBER	
EMAIL ADDRESS	
CONTACT METHOD	
NOTES	

NAME	
BIRTHDAY	
PHONE NUMBER	
EMAIL ADDRESS	
CONTACT METHOD	
NOTES	

NAME	
BIRTHDAY	
PHONE NUMBER	
EMAIL ADDRESS	
CONTACT METHOD	
NOTES	

NAME	
BIRTHDAY	
PHONE NUMBER	
EMAIL ADDRESS	
CONTACT METHOD	
NOTES	

NAME	
BIRTHDAY	
PHONE NUMBER	
EMAIL ADDRESS	
CONTACT METHOD	
NOTES	

NAME	
BIRTHDAY	
PHONE NUMBER	
EMAIL ADDRESS	
CONTACT METHOD	
NOTES	

NAME	
BIRTHDAY	
PHONE NUMBER	
EMAIL ADDRESS	
CONTACT METHOD	
NOTES	

NAME

BIRTHDAY	
PHONE NUMBER	
EMAIL ADDRESS	
CONTACT METHOD	

NOTES

NAME

BIRTHDAY	
PHONE NUMBER	
EMAIL ADDRESS	
CONTACT METHOD	

NOTES

NAME

BIRTHDAY	
PHONE NUMBER	
EMAIL ADDRESS	
CONTACT METHOD	

NOTES

attendance log

EXODUS 24-40 | A **SIMPLY BIBLE** STUDY

PARTICIPANT'S NAME	WEEK 1	WEEK 2	WEEK 3	WEEK 4	WEEK 5	WEEK 6	WEEK 7	WEEK 8	WEEK 9	WEEK 10
1										
2										
3										
4										
5										
6										
7										
8										
9										
10										
11										
12										
13										
14										
15										

prayer log

EXODUS 24-40 | A **SIMPLY BIBLE** STUDY

DATE	NAME	REQUEST	FOLLOW-UP

prayer log

EXODUS 24-40 | A **SIMPLY BIBLE** STUDY

DATE	NAME	REQUEST	FOLLOW-UP

prayer log

EXODUS 24-40 | A **SIMPLY BIBLE** STUDY

DATE	NAME	REQUEST	FOLLOW-UP

prayer log
EXODUS 24-40 | A **SIMPLY BIBLE** STUDY

DATE	NAME	REQUEST	FOLLOW-UP

prayer log

EXODUS 24-40 | A **SIMPLY BIBLE** STUDY

DATE	NAME	REQUEST	FOLLOW-UP

prayer log
EXODUS 24-40 | A **SIMPLY BIBLE** STUDY

DATE	NAME	REQUEST	FOLLOW-UP

prayer log

EXODUS 24-40 | A **SIMPLY BIBLE** STUDY

DATE	NAME	REQUEST	FOLLOW-UP

prayer log
EXODUS 24-40 | A **SIMPLY BIBLE** STUDY

DATE	NAME	REQUEST	FOLLOW-UP

And we know that for those who love God all things work together for good, for those who are called according to his purpose.

ROMANS 8:28

Made in the USA
Middletown, DE
12 February 2025